WEALTH –
GROW IT GOD'S WAY

DEENA MARIE CARR

ISBN: 0-9817608-0-5
978-0-9817608-0-3

Published by

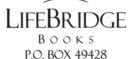
LIFEBRIDGE
B o o k s
P.O. BOX 49428
CHARLOTTE, NC 28277

Printed in the United States of America.

DEDICATION

*To my Dad: your memory
is present with me everyday.*

*To my Mom: without your strength, vision and
encouragement this book and so many other things
in my life would never have been. It is upon your
shoulders that I stand to reach for higher heights.*

*To my brother and sister: your unconditional
love has always encouraged me.*

*To my "Lil' Guy" Andrew, for whom
I work everyday: you have taught me
what selfless love truly is.*

3

CONTENTS

INTRODUCTION

While my great-grandfather was a Baptist minister, I was raised in the Pentecostal tradition after my mother's family migrated to Chicago and she converted. To fast forward to the punch-line, the result being that I was raised Pentecostal.

When I was growing up, one of the key pillars of this faith was an absolute belief and reliance on God. If they were sick, Pentecostals believed that Jesus was going to heal them, miraculously, if necessary. There were even those who did not believe in medical doctors at all. If they had a tumor or disease, they took "blessed oil" and prayed and trusted God to remove it. I was raised to understand that Jesus was the Great Physician. He was the "Lawyer in the Court Room." He was the "Bridge over Troubled Water."

This absolute faith in God translated to money and finances as well. Pentecostals did not really need money; they depended on God to always "make a way."

We "took no thought for tomorrow" because God was going to take care of us. We did not trust in earthly riches and human treasures, in fact, we knew that the love of these things was the root of all evil. Instead, we "laid up our treasures in heaven" in the form of faith and righteousness, because we understood that wherever our treasures were our hearts would also be (Matthew 6:19-21).

By the time my teenage years arrived, the "prosperity movement" was picking up steam. Money was no longer evil. In fact, it was the "in thing." God wanted us to be rich! Yes, absolutely and completely rich!

One of my favorite ministers said, "I have been rich and I have been poor, and rich is definitely better!" And while I in no way question that Jesus came so we might have life and that more abundantly, and while I believe "being the head and not the tail" is our spiritual birthright, I do believe we have to be wise in our extrapolations.

WHAT KIND OF RICHES?

Some seem to have concluded that this notion of "prosperity" translates into a law which states we are all supposed to be billionaires as a sign of God's favor—which seems to be little more akin to scriptural eisegesis than genuine logos revelation.

One of the things Jesus tried to teach the people during His time on earth was that they (and consequently "we") must understand the Lord God in a much broader context than simple "earthly riches." We must know God in the most important context of all—*spiritual riches.*

To me, you have to look no further than someone such as Mother Theresa who personified this when, as a nun, she "renounced wealth" to give her life in service to those less fortunate than herself. She was never wealthy but the impact of her life's work could probably be measured in billions.

This could be said for countless others, not the least of which being Dr. Martin Luther King. So the question is: *where is the balance between having a billion dollars and making a billion dollar impact?* And are the two concepts mutually exclusive?

When I talk about being raised in Pentecostalism, I do not highlight this as a way of celebrating what I think are unimportant differences in Christian pedagogical dogma. In fact, I believe the apostle Paul expressed it best when he said we should *"work out [our] own salvation with fear and trembling"* (Philippians 2:12); and that there is *"one body and one Spirit, just as [we were] called in one hope of [our] calling; one Lord, one faith, one baptism; one God and Father of all, who is above, and through all, and in [us] all* (Ephesians 4:4-6).

FAITH AND CULTURE

I share my experiences because I believe, like many people, my faith, the manner in which I was trained to relate to God, and my perspectives on how I serve the Lord was one of the biggest influences on a number of things in my life, including my viewpoints on money and wealth.

I feel that our belief systems about money are shaped by many things including our religious and cultural beliefs, our educational and life experiences. This takes me to the second "key influencer": my culture. Growing up in an African-American community, there was plenty of discussion concerning money, finance, economics, and wealth, but never from a place of holistic understanding or as empowered participants in a global economic system.

1. There were discussions about money, but those discussions were always concerning "how much money was required or how little money was available" to do what needed to be done.

2. There were discussions about finances, but "finances" usually only referred to the collection of bills one had, and whether or not he or she could pay them. If you could pay off all your bills, your "finances" were great. If you could not, your "finances" were bad. There were no discussions pertaining to the use of financial instruments to better structure and manage your cash flow or a portfolio of investments.

3. There were discussions about economics, but these were normally relagated to political leaders and pontificators talking on the socially unjust allocation of government resources to African-Americans.

"THE STRUGGLE"

In my world were no open discussions concerning wealth, how one created it, how much one had, and what strategies one used to increase or preserve it, because many of the African-Americans who had significant wealth often pretended as if they were "barely making it" themselves. Some may have done this to avoid being the victim of constant begging.

The secret of their wealth and the amount of their holdings grew into one big act of subterfuge—which could only be uncloaked during the feuds that ensued at their funerals. Another group may have pretended to be barely making it simply to fit in.

No one likes the feeling of being belittled because you could not identify with "The Struggle"; that would mean no longer being "black enough" and thus fully accepted. And then there were others who did not even bother to pretend; they instead chose to simply move away, change lifestyles, addresses, and numerous other things to become completely absorbed into a new world, more conducive to their higher socio-economic stratum.

AN ACADEMIC CHALLENGE

My next set of influences began with the study of economics. I took College Prep Economics my junior year at Whitney M. Young Magnet High School (named in one ranking as number two in the top high schools in the United States), in a class taught by David Dick.

This gifted teacher talked to us about concepts that were previously foreign to me such as "the economy," taxation, and real financing strategies. He did not care for simplistic discussions of corporate stocks, instead he wanted us to understand markets and the foundational principles of economics such as the allocation of scarce resources among unlimited wants.

This study and love of economics would continue and expand later at Northwestern University and the University of Chicago, challenging my Pentecostal African-American core with very profound alternative perspectives.

MERGING THE WORLDS

I was intrigued by the economic world because in this universe all people were "rational" and thus sought to maximize marginal utility and profitability and optimize "Pareto Efficiency." This is where, instead of being victims of the system, in the economic world, every rational person participated in a free market and was empowered to respond to, and even more importantly, influence the direction of market forces as they ebbed and shifted toward a stable "equilibrium" where all economic forces were "at one."

This probably began the temporary bifurcation of my faith world from my newly evolving financial world. In my religious upbringing, money did not matter; it was only marginally better than sin itself. In my financial world, I could always work to understand how to increase profits, assets, and ultimately wealth. My study of economics and finance was followed by years of work in the world of financial services: institutional money management, mergers and acquisition, benefits, insurance, investments, business strategy, and finally management consulting to some of Americas leading financial services corporations. Each facet of financial services provided a new window into the domain of wealth creation, wealth accumulation, wealth management, and wealth preservation. And each leg of the journey provided me with new perspectives, principles, and tools of how financial success is realized at both the individual and corporate level. But were they really new?

So all of these influences came together, my Christian upbringing, my African-American culture, my education, the years of work in the financial services industry. No longer was there a bifurcation between the faith world and the financial world. Instead, all of these aspects merged to ask the question, what is the role of financial wealth in the life of the believer? Is wealth only for those who do not believe? No, that does not seem even remotely consistent with the Bible and basic logic.

Should we consume ourselves striving to rabidly gain hordes of wealth? Well, that contradicts numerous scriptures in the Bible? So what is the role of wealth in the life of the believer?

SEEING WITH NEW EYES

This book is the result of my journey to understand how all of this fits together. I pray you will find it as helpful to you as it has been and continues to be to me. Our beliefs and experiences may vary slightly, but I am convinced that our shared belief in the Word of

God leads us to a common map for success. If we simply step back and look with a fresh set of eyes, we will see, like the famous psychology sketch, the picture is not of an old woman, but a young, vibrant woman full of personality and charm.

God has already outlined in His Word, the perfect way to build a healthy, balanced financial life: how to grow wealth—His way.

CHAPTER ONE

A BIBLICAL PERSPECTIVE ON WEALTH

THE CHRISTIAN DICHOTOMY

Definition: di·chot·o·my—something
with seemingly contradictory qualities.

O ne of the things that I have experienced and
observed throughout life is the phenomenon I refer to
as the *Christian Dichotomy.* On one hand, as
believers, we desire to make money and have
abundance so we can easily take care of ourselves, our
loved ones, and our progeny for generations to come.
On the other hand, we do not want to have so much
wealth that we forget God, building massive barns to
store our vast earthly treasures—completely, losing our
souls on the way to amassing the great fortunes of this
world.

Yes, we feel the need to be wise and follow

15

Proverbs 6:6—being like the ant who stores food for lean times. However, we do not want to be so consumed in providing for ourselves that we forget: *"Unless the Lord build the house, they labor in vain who build it"* (Psalm 127:1).

We want to always remember that we do not have to "take any thought for tomorrow" for just as the Lord "clothes the lily of the fields" and "feeds the ravens," He will do even more for us.

So where in this tug of war is the balance? What is the proper amount of wealth? What is too much? How do we focus on increasing money without falling in love with it?

For me, the answer to these questions are extremely important because we cannot expect to maximize the potential God has placed in us regarding building wealth until we are sure we can and *will* remain in the perfect will of God as we obtain success.

I once heard a speaker say, "A person will always strive to remain true to his or her inner core values—his or her inner self."

As believers in Christ Jesus, this is particularly true in our lives, especially when we embark upon the topic of wealth. Over the years, as I have talked with people about finances, I have seen this struggle to remain consistent with our core values time and time again.

One person may sit down and make their plans for building great fortune in the future. While another person says, "You know, I really don't want to be rich. I have no desire to accumulate too much money. I just want enough to be comfortable."

At first glance, this person who only wants to be comfortable may seem like an "underachiever." In fact, some of you may be tempted to say that he or she is completely and thoroughly indolent and trifling. But in almost every situation, the rationale that the person gives is more akin to Proverbs 30:7-9 than anything else. Their position is sound Biblical position.

> *Two things I ask of you, O Lord; do not refuse me before I die: Keep falsehood and lies far from me; give me neither poverty nor riches, but give me only my daily bread. Otherwise, I may have too much and disown you and say, 'Who is the Lord?' Or I may become poor and steal, and so dishonor the name of my God* (NIV).

In effect, they desire to balance the seemingly opposing forces—to reconcile the apparent contradiction between desiring some amount of wealth to be effective but wanting to avoid the level of riches that causes one to lose their soul. So how do we move beyond this dichotomy?

The answer is "very prayerfully." First, we must understand God's definition of wealth, as outlined in scripture. And second, we must comprehend our responsibility as Christians regarding how we manage that wealth.

WHAT DOES GOD WANT?

We must begin by considering this basic question: Does God want us to be wealthy?

Think about it, and do not give a super-spiritual answer. Sure, the Bible says, *"I pray that you may prosper in all things and be in health, just as your soul prospers"* (3 John 1:2). We all know that. We also understand that Jesus said He came that we would have life and that more abundantly (John 10:10). So, we cannot deny the holistic properties of wealth discussed in the Bible, but right now I want to be very specific and talk about wealth strictly in terms of financial riches.

Do you actually believe that God wants us, His children, to be *financially* wealthy in *this* life?

WEALTH BY WINNING?

For those of us who have a neo-Pentecostal orientation, we definitely believe God wants us to be wealthy, because we pray for the Lord to send checks in the mail all of the time! This is our definition of wealth: just believing in God and hoping for the money to flow out of nowhere. We also believe there is going to come a day where we are walking down the street and money is just going to suddenly appear; it's going to fall right out of the sky! That's wealth for us.

My personal favorite—and you probably have

never prayed this prayer, but I used to—was to pray that someone would just give me a winning lottery ticket.

Today, however, because of what I read in scripture, I don't play the lottery. Proverbs 13:11 speaks of the dangers of wealth quickly gotten. And we have read the horror stories involving the lives of many lottery winners.

Yet, you see those mega jackpots, and it's tempting to pray, "Wouldn't it be great if I found a winning lottery ticket?"

Even with the potential pitfalls of money, and even though we know there is only a slight chance of winning, it's still potential wealth for us, so we put faith in the chance that we will actual win.

However, this win-big lottery scenario isn't the type of wealth that I am talking about; I am speaking of the wealth that is actually sustaining, that produces an income, allows us to live a life that is exciting and fulfilled, and, most important, allows us to extend the Kingdom of God.

Think about it again. Does God want us to be wealthy?

The answer is *Yes*, God does want us to be wealthy, but it is not the lottery winning, riverboat gambling, or overnight riches that we focus on. The Lord is specific about wealth. He defines it, gives His children the ability to acquire it, and presents specific instructions on how to manage it.

WEALTH DEFINED
(FOUR TYPES OF WEALTH)

One of the major lessons I learned is that to avoid the feelings I discussed in the section on the Christian Dichotomy, I must keep my focus on God without becoming consumed with what is superficial. I had to look at wealth from God's perspective and not my own.

In Deuteronomy 8, God addresses the children of Israel before they go into the Promised Land. He takes time to remind them that their obedience and remembrance of God is tantamount as they enter this territory and begin to receive His promised wealth.

The Almighty then enumerates what the wealth is:

> *Therefore you shall keep the commandments of the Lord your God, to walk in His ways and to fear Him. For the Lord your God is bringing you in a **(1) good land,** a land of brooks of water, of fountains and springs, that flow out of valleys and hills; a land of wheat and barley, of vines and fig trees and pomegranates, a land of olive oil and honey; a land in which you will eat bread without scarcity, in which you will lack nothing; a land whose stones are iron and out of whose hills you can dig copper.*
>
> *Beware that you do not forget the Lord your God by not keeping His commandments, His*

judgments, and His statutes which I command
you today, lest – when you have eaten and are
full, and have (2) built beautiful houses and
dwell in them; and when your (3) herds and
your flocks multiply, and your (4) silver and
your gold are multiplied, and all that you have
is multiplied; when your heart is lifted up, and
you forget the Lord your God who brought you
out of the land of Egypt, from the house of
bondage....

And you shall remember the Lord your God,
for it is He who gives you the power to get
wealth, that He may establish His covenant
which He swore to your fathers, as it is this day"
(Deuteronomy 8:6-14,18).

God was fairly comprehensive concerning the type
of wealth the children of Israel would realize. He
described four types: land, houses, herds and flocks,
silver and gold. I would like to consider each of these
in modern terms.

1. Land: Modern day equivalent = A defined parcel of land.

This is an easy one! God was not promising the
children of Israel a figurative Promised Land, but a
specific location they could occupy; a good place that
had an ample supply of water, food, and other vital
resources.

Today, we can see how land still is valuable. With
the world's population continuing to increase, land is

not only vital for habitation, but it is important because of what it can produce. The land yields food which feeds people all around the world.

In June 2008 the United Nation's Food and Agriculture Organization gathered in Rome for a summit on how to address the world's current food crisis. The conclave included debates on how they could increase the output of land to produce the food needed all over the globe. How could this be done in a way that avoided destroying other vital land resources such as the rain forests?

Land also gives us access to or allows us to take out valuable resources such as bauxite, coal, diamonds, iron ore, and copper. In fact, in Deuteronomy 8:9, God spoke of *"a land whose stones are iron and out of whose hills you can dig copper."*

So my question to you is: When you pray and ask the Lord to increase you, do you pray for land? I am not referring only to the earth that would be a part of a home purchase. I am speaking of owning land where commercial enterprises can be established. Do you think about land for a bigger dream, a larger mission? Allow me to give you two examples.

One of the things that struck me about Walt Disney is that after he built Disneyland in Anaheim, California, he had a dream to create something even better. To accomplish his new vision, he needed land—and lots of it!

He and his team began searching for land throughout America until he finally settled on some swampland in Orlando, Florida, and went about secretly purchasing the parcels at approximately $180 per acre. Later, when people found out that Disney was buying the land, its price soared to more than $1000 per acre. Even though Disney died before the new theme park, Disney World, was created, in a few short years, the land he bought was transformed into one of the greatest attractions ever.

Decades later, people from all over the world still travel to Disney World and other Disney attractions. His dream was put into motion with the purchase of land.

So here is a homework question for you. What is Disney's land worth today?

Another example concerning the importance of land can be seen in business transactions all around the world where corporations and even governments are making deals to purchase land which allows them to mine or extract important resources.

Each year billions of dollars of *deals* are completed for land and land-related enterprises. According to Bloomberg News' October 21st, 2007 report, Chinaco paid $860 million in a deal for PeruCopper.

The exact type of wealth God promised His children, thousands of years later, it is still proving to be valuable to mankind.

2. Houses: Modern day equivalent = Property.

Most of us have a desire to own a home. And some of us desire to own *multiple* properties: summer homes, vacations homes, and condos in places like the

South of France. (Personally, I'd like a home in the South Pacific. The South Island of New Zealand or Fiji would be just perfect).

But the question I would like to ask is: have our desires extended beyond our own personal home ownership, to the ownership of different types of property, such as residential apartment complexes, commercial buildings or industrial properties? Have we thought of Monopoly as more than just a game, but as a list of things that we can own? Housing developments, hotels, power companies, railroads, should be just a few of the things that come to mind. And all of these and more are examples of opportunities we have today to build wealth. And it is consistent with the wealth God spoke of to His children.

Many years ago, I worked for a company that was involved in a number of really interesting projects, not the least of which was masterminding complex financing transactions for large investment purchases such as nuclear power plants and huge real estate holdings.

When I first learned what the company did, I was fascinated because the idea of financing something like a power plant had never crossed my mind. It was a completely foreign concept to me. I guess I thought that because a power company could be granted a monopoly by a local government, somehow "the government" just magically provided them with a facility and everything they needed to conduct business.

I don't know if this was just basic naïveté' or if it was my "God will send a check in the mail" mentality on autopilot. But working for the company, I learned that individuals like you and me, were putting together multi-million dollar and billion dollar deals all of the time, with complex structures such as Sale-Leasebacks to provide power companies with the money they needed to build a new nuclear power facility.

These people were also developing malls all over the country. Wow, I did not know that was possible. I thought "companies" built the malls, and they did. But, the little fact that escaped me previously was that companies were made up of people like me!

These individuals had found a different way to "be blessed." They used their intelligence, their network, and their perseverance to participate in America's free enterprise system on an entirely different level.

Through this experience I began to see how God provides His children with the ability to be blessed in ways far greater than I had ever imagined. What is beyond your imagination? Have you limited God in terms of what is really possible in your future?

I was intrigued by the news on June 10, 2008. There was quite a discussion on one of the U.S. business news channels regarding the proposed takeover of one the nation's largest railroads, CSX, by a foreign hedge fund (TCI). For some it was a matter of national security to challenge the possible ownership of a national asset by a foreign entity.

While I believe that every nation's security is paramount, including my own, I could not help being impressed by the *gutsiness* of this firm. They were not limiting themselves in anyway regarding what was possible. They saw what they believed was a marvelous business opportunity and they were going for it. Do we, with our awesome faith, demonstrate an equivalent level of ingenuity and courage?

3. Herds and Flocks: Modern day equivalent = Businesses and Corporations.

Perhaps you are wondering where I am going with the "herds and flocks" metaphor. Even with food shortages around the world making farming and livestock related businesses more lucrative, you may still say to yourself, "This is not my life's aspiration." But I think there is a great deal we can learn.

A simple perusal of a resource such as *Wikipedia* tells us that shepherding thousands of years ago was a grueling job. A shepherd was typically a wage employee, paid to oversee the *flocks of others*.

Interesting! In Deuteronomy 8:13, the Lord specifically says *"when your herds and flocks"* are multiplied.

In the Promised Land, God's children are no longer the employees—they are the owners! What type of business do you want to own or invest in?

4. Silver and Gold: Modern day equivalent = Precious Metals and enduring mediums of exchange.

Even today, silver and gold have value. Let's look

at gold. According to the London Bullion Market Association[1], from June 1 2000 to June 2, 2008, the price of gold per troy ounce in U.S. dollars grew from $280.35 to $891.25. Not including the various points during 2008 where the price per troy ounce crossed $1000, a price of $891 means that gold has more than tripled in value in just eight short years, providing investors with a compound annual growth rate over 16% per year.

Precious Metals	Price ($per oz)	Date of Prices
Silver	$ 16.55	June 13, 2008
Palladium	$ 451	June 13, 2008
Rhuthenium	$ 425	March 2008*
Iridium	$ 450	March 2008
Platinum	$ 2,036	June 13, 2008
Rhodium	$ 9,050	March 2008

*Source: Johnson Matthey Precious Metals Marketing

Gold and silver are part of a broader category known as precious metals. I believe the Lord was telling the children of Israel that in the Promised Land they could expect to see all kinds of precious metals of enduring quality and value. Today resources continue to be valuable and there are several to choose from.

A major U.S. credit card company asks the question at the end of their television commercials, "What's in your wallet?"

Looking at the value of precious metals makes me

---

[1] Daily AM prices for London Gold Fixing: London Bullion Market Association.

ask the same question. Hopefully it's a certificate for the purchase of a few ounces of Rhodium!

But there is one more thing we can take away from the type of wealth described. Silver and gold also served as currency during the time the children of Israel entered into the Promised Land. Until 1971, when the U.S. abandoned the Bretton Woods system, gold still served as the store value for currency in our nation. Post 1971, however, the U.S. moved to a floating currency system.

According to a March 7, 2008 speech by Federal Reserve governor Frederic Mishkin in Oslo Norway, since 2002, the U.S. dollar "has depreciated over 40 percent against a basket of major currencies, weighted by their countries' trade with the United States."

With this type of currency depreciation, it is encouraging to see that the children of Israel would have a medium of exchange with more enduring value.

WEALTH POWER

So if we agree that God wants us to be wealthy, and that He defined some of the types of wealth we could expect, let me highlight a factor I believe is extremely important. In Deuteronomy 8:18, the Lord says He is the one who gives *"the power"* to attain wealth.

If we read this very carefully, we notice God does not say, I am the one who *gives you* the wealth, instead, He was very careful to point out, "I am the one who gives you the *power* to get wealth."

Remember, the Almighty was moving the children of Israel, the people of promise, from a place where they had to look to heaven for their daily bread to a land where they could provide for themselves and develop self-sufficiency (being self-sufficient in that it was already divinely appointed).

This is where we want to be. We believe God made an everlasting covenant with Abraham and that through Jesus Christ, who came down from heaven and reconciled us back to the Father, we are joint-heirs to all God promised.

When we look carefully, we see that wealth is not the beautiful clothes, hats, or shoes we wear. It is not even the fancy cars we drive. These things are all wonderful, but that is exactly what they are— "things."

I believe God has placed in us an internal alarm system and when we become lost in the pursuit of things, our alarm goes off and tells us that we are not on the right path. We are not building what is of value, what really matters.

To build Godly wealth is to accumulate resources with enduring value and perpetual income streams. Now if I decide to build a portfolio of "things" (especially if I use credit cards in the process), instead of building a wealth portfolio, I have the power to make that choice.

Looking at it another way, I can spend my prayer time asking God to help me get out of one bad decision (and/or debt) after another or I can spend my prayers asking for guidance in how to build Kingdom wealth. My power. My choice.

THE RESPONSIBILITY OF WEALTH

No discussion about the Bible and finances is complete without at least a passing reference to the Parable of the Talents found in Matthew 25. Regardless of how many times we read this passage of scripture or how often we hear ministers expound on the story, we always receive a little more insight and motivation to maximize our potential in God with each encounter.

I would like to return to this passage to highlight three keys I believe are critical if we are to build wealth God's way.

One, this parable, according to Jesus, was about the Kingdom of God. It is interesting to note that the Lord used *a parable about money* to explain to His followers the mysteries of the Kingdom. The "money" issue is sometimes overlooked because the popular translation of scripture uses the word talent.

A "talent" was equal to a particular amount of money. We could compound the sum to calculate the value in today's dollars, but some may not find that remotely interesting. So let's simply say that a talent was equal to a days wages.

It is easy to look at talents in terms of the natural and spiritual gifts that God has bestowed upon us, but I believe Jesus deliberately used a parable about money so that we can extract the financial lessons as well as the spiritual lessons that are critical to understanding the mysteries of the Kingdom of God.

The second key is that we must realize everyone is not going to be entrusted with the same level of wealth, whether spiritual, natural or financial. We must come to terms with this, because perhaps some people imagine they are going have Bill Gates' riches or Oprah Winfrey's stock portfolio simply because they love Jesus and obey His Word.

No matter how faithful you are and no matter how much you love Jesus, it's about the Lord first. He knows how much we need to do what He has called us to accomplish. Luke recounts Jesus saying that each one is given according to his or her ability.

This last point leads me to what I feel is perhaps the most crucial lesson of all for the believer. *No matter what our level of wealth, we have a responsibility to manage it to the best of our ability and to increase it.*

Some people believe that wealth does not begin until you reach some preset level. But wealth is like a child, it is entrusted to us, and because of that, we have an obligation to manage it as effectively as we can and to help it increase. It doesn't matter if we only have $25 dollars, that is enough. With faith, prayer, wisdom and diligence, we can increase it. If God has entrusted us with more, maybe $25 million, it doesn't matter, we cannot rest there, we have a responsibility to put that money to work and make it grow.

We often criticize famous people who we feel don't do enough with their charitable giving. However, it does not matter whether you are a celebrity or not; when you are entrusted with wealth, there is more responsibility to preserve and grow it.

THE PURPOSE OF WEALTH

The real question is: what are we growing our money *for?*

We must tap into the fact that the purpose of our wealth is not just so we can be comfortable in this life. The Bible tells us, *"You ask and do not receive, because you ask amiss, that you may spend it on your pleasures"*(James 4:3). The reason we increase our wealth is so we can do more to make a difference in the Kingdom on God.

In the same chapter of Matthew 25 (verses 32-45), Jesus shares another parable of how people were sick, in prison, and hungry, and nothing was done about it. The lesson is that when we do things for the least in our society, we have done it for the Lord.

We use this scripture as a mandate to expand our charitable efforts around the world, which I think is absolutely fantastic. Wealth is desperately needed to fund these efforts. But, we can't stop there. We must build infrastructures and perpetual institutions (i.e., the businesses promised in Deuteronomy 8) that solve the issues that plague our society once and for all.

We can't just wait until the imminent return of the Messiah for all these things to miraculously go away. And it is not the government's responsibility to fix these problems. It is the duty and obligation of His children. He told us that we are supposed to do even greater things than He did. Jesus healed the sick, caused the blind to see, the deaf to hear, and He raised the dead. To do even more is a tall order, but this is what we have been commissioned to do.

A CULTURAL QUESTION

So far, we have been talking about wealth and the power God gives us to have financial abundance. Allow me to address in particular my African-American brothers and sisters. The question I want you to consider is, if you believe God has ordained us to be wealthy, why aren't there more wealthy African-Americans? It's truly something to ponder, and obviously, there is much thought that needs to be put into addressing this complex question.

Let's assume for a moment that everyone in the United States is a Christian. I am not saying everyone has to be a Christian—of course, I want everyone to be—but let's just pretend it is true. Why am I starting with this assumption? I know that in any science or discipline, when you are trying to solve a difficult equation, you begin by assuming away the difficult aspects of the problem so that you can solve it.

This, for example, is how economists come to really solid conclusions; they assume away obscure things in order to draw amazing insights. So we are going to assume that everyone in the United States is a Christian. According to statistics, African-Americans make up roughly 12% of the population, yet they have only about 2% of the wealth. Do you believe that God loves some of His children more than others?

I, for one, do not. I believe He has given all Christians the power to gain wealth. But here we have a situation where some Christians, the African-American ones, have less wealth than other Christians, and this does not seem right to me.

MOVING TO THE NEXT LEVEL

The easy answer to our question would come, in part,from recognizing a difficult history of oppression. However,let me throw some more statistics at you. I'll give you some exact numbers which reveal something rather interesting:

- In 2000, the net worth of white Christians (because in my example, we assume everyone is a Christian) was about $79,000.
- The net worth of black Christians was only $7,500.

Net worth is calculated as all of the stuff you own less all the stuff you owe. Some believers had $79,000 of net worth, and others had only $7,500. Looking at these numbers, I said to myself, "This does not seem right."But, even as I stared at the cold, hard truth, produced by the U.S. census, it said something quite revealing.

Black and Hispanic households hold a significantly higher proportion of their net worth in durable goods, i.e., houses and cars.

Now, we all know that cars do not increase in value over time (unless they are classic automobiles or some sort of collector's vehicle). The census report also tells us that black and Hispanic (Christian) households have a significantly lower proportion of their financial resources in stocks, mutual funds, and interest-bearing assets at financial institutions, and this is also true for their 401(K) retirement plans and IRAs.

So certain Christians do not own the types of wealth that seem to be what the Lord talks about in Deuteronomy (land, homes, herds and flocks, and silver and gold). He wants to give us all these things, yet we are buying cars. We're not actually building the type of wealth we could be.

Yes, we are doing fairly well with buying houses, but what about the land and the businesses? What about taking it to the next level? God wants us to move up a notch, where we actually are wealthy and financially independent—and where most of our prayers are not for God to pay our bills, deliver us from debt, or prevent us from losing our jobs.

It's time to move to the next plateau, where we have the type of wealth that allows us to focus our prayer on how the Lord can direct us in reaching people who are hurting, reconciling the disenfranchised, restoring hope, and overall, making an indelible impression on the world for Christ.

FOOD FOR THOUGHT

I discovered a couple of other points related to the

highest and lowest percentages of ownership, and found that approximately 51% of the people who were in the top 20% of income earners owned stock. If you look at the bottom 20%, less than 10% owned stock.

I do not know what category you are in, but if you don't own any stocks or similar wealth-building vehicles,there is a higher probability that you are going to correspond to the bottom performers as opposed to the top performers.

We can also examine other areas, such as what percentage of Christians own businesses. Sixty percent of the people who are really making money and creating wealth own a business of some sort.

God wants us to remember that we have been blessed with businesses, as He promised in Deuteronomy, but when we develop these enterprises, we shouldn't think we did it by ourselves —it was He who gave us the ability and power.

Well, if we are afraid to start a business because it's hard work and many new commercial ventures fail, are we operating from a point of faith, or are we functioning from a point of fear?

What are we doing with the power He gave us? Sometimes God wants you to start a business because He is trying to create some flexibility and take you to another level of wealth that you may not have been able to experience on your own.

I am not against jobs, but at times a nine-to-five occupation can be a constraint, and you cannot do all the Lord wants you to do because you are bound by the responsibilities and laws of your assigned position.

If you are unwilling to try a new avenue because of ignorance or if you have fear instead of faith, then the enemy can keep you bound—and that is really the point.

We have to break free. We need to raise our consciousness in terms of what wealth truly is, and we can start by asking God not for a parking space but for the true blessing to do something powerful.

If we choose not to be persuaded by what we see or hear on the news, not to be intimidated by the fact we feel there is an entire section of the newspaper we just can't understand, and instead truly tap into the reality we can build wealth no matter how young or old we are, we will see that God truly has given each of us the power to create wealth.

MAKING A DIFFERENCE

Wealth does not begin in the natural; it begins in the spiritual. This is because wealth ultimately comes from and belongs to God. All you are doing is exercising your spiritual muscle to become one of His stewards.

Jesus said, *"The harvest truly is plentiful, but the laborers are few"* (Matthew 9:37).

I don't think laborers exist just so we can all become preachers. I believe the Lord needs some individuals to have wealth because there are people in the world who are suffering, and these men, women and children need spiritual solutions—but they also need financial solutions.

The Kingdom is waiting for people like you and me, who understand that God has given us enough power to be as prosperous as He has ordained for us to be, so that we can make a difference.

I also believe this is why the teachings of Jesus concerning wealth seemed slightly different from those ideas we read in the Old Testament.

The Jews understood the promises given to their forefathers and prophets regarding riches and possessions, but Jesus emphasized that salvation was based on the heart of man, and our focus should be beyond the accumulation of wealth; it should be on building the Kingdom of God. It should be centered on doing all that we can to make a difference, and if wealth, no matter how large or small, does not serve that purpose, it is of no use.

CHAPTER TWO

KEEPING YOUR LIFE IN BALANCE

In the previous chapter, we started building a foundational understanding of wealth using the Bible as our guide. We will continue to expand our view, but first I want to digress and talk about the importance of being balanced in our approach to wealth, finances or put more directly—money!

Let me start with the disclaimer that this is not the "name it, claim it" superspiritual approach to wealth, where you simply lay hands on your wallets and purses, and dollars just spontaneously materialize. That's the easy way! Here, we are talking about *actual work and effort.*

Sure, in the past we may have seen ourselves like the children of Israel in the wilderness. They woke up every morning, and before them was *manna*. This was truly miraculous; they exerted *no effort, except to wake up.*

Wouldn't it be great if we arose every day to find our own fresh bread (money) from heaven?

We lose sight of the fact that God supplied the

manna during this period He was preserving them—literally and figuratively. Scripture records, "*I have led you forty years in the wilderness. Your clothes have not worn out on you, and your sandals have not worn out on your feet*" (Deuteronomy 29:5).

When it was eventually time for them to go and possess the Promised Land, as we said earlier, God no longer provided them with manna; instead, He gave them *power*—the power to get wealth, among other things. The Lord follows this same model later.

When Jesus left the disciples and returned to the Father, He left them with power—power in the form of The Comforter, the Holy Spirit. The challenge for us is: *how do we appropriately use this power in every area of living, especially in our financial lives?*

KEEP YOUR LIFE IN FINANCIAL BALANCE

Over the years I have observed and talked with many who struggle with money issues—often the lack of it, at other times, the "proper acquisition" of it. In the process I have noticed some consistent thinking patterns or what I will refer to as "thinking imbalances."

Imbalance #1: Praying and fasting alone will solve all of my financial problems.

Some believe that the holy actions of praying and fasting are what will move them to wealth. Don't get me wrong: I wholeheartedly believe in prayer and fasting as well as the nine gifts of the Spirit. I grew up in a home where these two actions were pillars to our faith and survival. And while, to this day, I still pray and petition God daily for financial guidance and sometimes even intervention, the Lord has taught me that prayer and fasting alone will not build the wealth that He has appointed for me to build.

Financial abundance is created not just by faith but by actions and by works.

I am reminded of these words in the second epistle of James:

> *What does it profit, my brethren, if someone says he has faith but does not have works? Can faith save him? If a brother or sister is naked and destitute of daily food, and one of you says to them, "Depart in peace, be warmed and filled, "but you do not give them the things which are needed for the body, what does it profit? Thus also faith by itself, if it does not have works, is dead. But someone will say, "you have faith, and I works."*
>
> *Show me your faith without your works, and I will show you my faith by my works. You believe that there is one God. You do well. Even the demons believe—and tremble! But do you want to know, O foolish man, that faith without works is dead? Was not Abraham our father justified by works when he offered Isaac his son on the altar?*
>
> *Do you see that faith was working together with his works, and by faith was made perfect?*

And the Scripture was fulfilled which says, "Abraham believed God, and it was accounted to him for righteousness, and he was called the friend of God (James 2:14-23).

Yes, we draw upon our spiritual grounding to help us in every area of our lives, including our finances. Our faith leads us, as Philippians 4:6 says, to avoid being *"…anxious about anything, but in everything, by prayer and petition, with thanksgiving, present your requests to God."*

Prayer, supplication, and thanksgiving are all absolutely essential. This *is* faith. But then we combine our faith with actions—with works—to *bring about results.*

Imbalance #2: Positive speaking alone will produce wealth.

Here's another action that will not create financial abundance by itself—simply declaring it. I have heard many refer to the scripture that tells us to speak those things that are not as though they were (Romans 4:17). So they go around saying, "I'm rich! I'm rich! I'm a millionaire! I'm a billionaire!"

I do believe Proverbs 23:7 which tells us, *"For as [a man] thinks in his heart, so is he."* I also adhere to the truth of Proverbs 18:21: *"Death and life are in the power of the tongue, and those who love it will eat its fruit."*

If we speak negatively, negative things will happen. It is as if the *"principalities"* and *"powers"* the apostle

Paul talks about in Ephesians 6:12 are emboldened by negative confessions.

Instead, we should speak positively. We should speak life—energizing our lives by addressing the invisible as though it is visible. But we cannot stop there; we must add works.

I am reminded of a humorous story my mother used to tell about the days when she was new in seminary. She said she thought the Holy Ghost was going to study for her. All she had to do was simply lay the Bible on her head, speak in tongues, and when she went in to take the exam, she would score an A.

Much to her dismay, this technique did not work.

Then she said the Holy Ghost quietly whispered to her, "Thus saith the Lord God: Study."

The same principle applies to our finances. I don't want to sound cynical, because I truly, truly love the Lord, but I have seen and heard so many mystical messages and confessions, accompanied by individuals "laying hands on their money" and "pouring blessed oil" on their finances—numerous rituals over material things. Sometimes, I feel like shouting, "Thus saith the Lord God: study, practice, work the principles that He laid out in His word*!*" *[You have to say it in old English because it makes it sound more official.]*

We must roll up our sleeves and *build* wealth step by step.

I want to repeat this until it is etched in our consciousness. In Deuteronomy 8, the Lord never said to the children of Israel that He wanted them to remember that it was He who *gave* them the wealth.

In fact, in verses 17-18, God declared, "Do not say that it was *your* power and strength that produced riches, but it was the power and strength that *I gave to YOU* to produce the wealth."

To realize these kinds of results means we have to study and we have to work. If we do not put our mind, words and energy toward the activities and investments which produce wealth, we cannot expect God to bless us with these things.

Imbalance #3: We must live from one miraculous gift to the other.

God Promises He will give us *"wells which you did not dig [and vineyards and olive trees which you did not plant"* (Deuteronomy 6:12). These are miracles, but the Bible also tells us we must sow before we reap.

Too many are looking for the blessings that come without effort. While this can be a part of our Christian experience, the Lord does not want us to structure our financial lives so that we have to live from one miracle to the next. In the Promised Land, the Lord describes how the children of Israel would be *abiding in a place of wealth.* The only thing that could mess up this sustained position was if they forgot God and disobeyed.

Abundance was not a condition that just happened to them and lasted for only a moment—and then they waited for the same manifestation to occur again and again. No, when God blesses, He sends His favor *on a sustained level.*

We must recognize the fact that our Father desires

for us to be blessed *continually.* And, if we seek Him, He will show us how to use our power (the power granted to us by Him) to create the types of wealth that sustain ourselves and others for years to come.

Imbalance #4: A sign of God's blessing on our lives is the amount of things we have.

We take our faith and put it to work in order to build wealth. The purpose is not so we can buy our own jet, or yacht, or private island in the Mediterranean. I'm sure we all would like something like that—I know I would. We may very well have all of these possessions, and more, some day. But acquiring "things" is not really the purpose of wealth.

Let me say it this way: *it is not the mission of our wealth.* Our true mission is to make a difference in the Kingdom of God. The finances can help us be a blessing, so that when we see needs, we can take from that which God has entrusted to us and make an impact.

View it from this perspective: Your mission in life is not to buy a state-of-the-art high-definition plasma television with a Blue Ray DVD player. No, your divine calling may be to administer medicine to heal people suffering with Parkinson's disease. Along the way, you may buy a plasma TV, but it is not your mission. The objective of your wealth is tied directly to your God-given purpose on this earth. The two (your mission and your wealth) are intrinsically woven together.

Be about your Father's business and He will be about yours!

FORTY ACRES AND A MULE

Before we move ahead, I would like to share one more word with my African-American brothers and sisters.

I believe one of the most negative results which can befall people who have gone through oppression is that the experience can produce a lingering belief system of powerlessness that is passed down through the generations.

African-American ancestors fought slavery through perseverance and an unfailing belief that as God delivered the children of Israel, surely He would deliver them. Later in the Jim Crow South, African Americans fought discrimination through passive resistance and the infectious belief deep in their heart that they would overcome.

Now, in the twenty-first century, with so many opportunities available to us, ones our ancestors could only dream of, too many of us are still waiting for a savior to come and *give* us wealth. We are simply waiting to be granted the 40 acres and a mule!

You see, like the theologian James Cone, I believe that *God is the God of the oppressed.* I also am convinced that one of the miracles the Lord performs on the downtrodden is to free and to restore them to a state of empowerment.

Once we are brought back to a place of power, with our heavenly Father's guidance, we have the ability to acquire everything else we need and desire. We do not have to wait for anyone to give us anything.

Let me put this in economic terms, my favorite. We learn from Economics 101 that if we were to define the market for any goods or service in terms of price paid and quantity supplied, equilibrium occurs at the point where P (price) equals Q (quantity). Equilibrium (E^*) is important because it is the only place where everything is stable.

We also learn that for various reasons, situations can occur where price and quantity are not aligned. This is called disequilibrium, and it is not a sustainable position. Whenever there is disequilibrium, *ceteris paribus* (all things being equal), market forces will always act to return the market to a state of equilibrium (E^*). It is only at this point that the market can be in a steady state.

I believe the same thing happens with God's people. To be powerless or oppressed is a state of disequilibrium. The Lord will always intervene to restore His people to a place of empowerment.

YOUR AUTHORITY

Allow me to go further by saying that Jesus left His throne in Glory to redeem man from the *oppression* of sin. Before He ascended back to the Father, He said, *"All authority in heaven and on earth has been given to me"* (Matthew 28:18).

Then, in the very next verse Jesus gave that power to us: *"Therefore go and make disciples of all nations, baptizing them in the name of the Father and of the Son and of the Holy Spirit, and teaching them to obey everything I have commanded you"* (verses 19-20).

The purpose of redemption was to reconcile humankind back to the Father and, thus, to restore us to a place of power. Once in our rightful role of authority, the next step is to use the power to show the glory of God. For example:

- *"Then He called His twelve disciples together and gave them power and authority over all demons, and to cure diseases"* (Luke 9:1).

- *"But you shall receive power when the Holy Spirit has come upon you; and you shall be witnesses to Me in Jerusalem, and in all Judea and Samaria, and to the end of the earth"* (Acts 1:8).

- *"And with great power the apostles gave witness to the resurrection of the Lord Jesus. And great grace was upon them all"* (Acts 4:33).

- *"But we have this treasure in earthen vessels, that the excellence of the power may be of God and not of us"* (2 Corinthians 4:7).

- *"Now to him who is able to do exceedingly abundantly above all that we ask or think, according to the power that works in us"* (Ephesians 3:20).

To further bring this point home, I believe as previously oppressed[1] people, we have seen too many of our hopes and dreams for wealth being dashed because of doors slammed in our faces or deals mysteriously not coming through.

Too many of us have become discouraged from taking the risks required because of the past failures and exploitations. In the process, the muscles we used to fight and to build wealth have atrophied. And still, for too many others, we have never even tried to create wealth because generations before us, our grandfathers, grandmothers, great-uncles, and great-aunts, became convinced it was impossible.

As a result, from the time we were children, we were taught to see God only as a "barely enough" provider. If folks truly wanted to be rich, they had to leave the church to do so.

But I am here to tell you that God has given *all* of us power, and there is no more urgent a time than the present to use it. Around the world, people are hurting and suffering. We need to help them.

If we tap into the fact that God has given us the authority and power, we do not have to become intimidated or feel left out. We don't even have to get puffed up with arrogance and feel it was our great

---

[1] Some would argue that there is still a great deal of overt and, even more, covert oppression of African-Americans. My point is not to debate whether oppression exists but to emphasize the fact that the Lord has given us enough power to do His perfect will in our lives.

education or brilliant insight that produced wealth.

When we are successful, we know it is because of His power at work in us.

CHAPTER THREE

DEFINING WEALTH IN SIMPLE TERMS

Earlier we talked about the type of wealth that God promised the children of Israel. I would like to return to this discussion and specifically agree on a definition and measure of financial wealth. This will serve as the basis for future discussions in subsequent chapters, as we continue to use the principles of the Bible to "grow wealth God's way."

Many look at this as a nebulous term, but let's "make it plain." Wealth is quite simply "stuff." But, it's not just *any* stuff, instead it is made up of those kinds of things that hold or increase in value.

The technical financial term for this is an asset. My definition of an asset is: *something that increases in value (continually over time) and preferably provides us with a perpetual income, either now or in the future.*

So, you might conclude, "All I have to do to be wealthy is acquire a lot of assets. Right?" This would be partially true but it would not be the entire answer.

CALCULATING NET WORTH

Over the years, I have seen a number of people who go about life accumulating a lot of things, some of which would fit our definition of assets, but not all. As a result of what they have accumulated, they feel as though they are doing rather well. But, if we take a closer look, we see that they are not really succeeding to the extent they may have originally thought. In some cases, perhaps they are even struggling to make ends meet. Why? Because in their pursuit of "things," they amassed quite a bit of financial overhead, also known as *liabilities*. These are *financial obligations such as short and long term debt.*

So the true measure of wealth is not just the total amount of assets that we have, but it also includes the total amount of liabilities. I refer to this as the *Net Wealth calculation*, but the formal financial term is *Net Worth*.

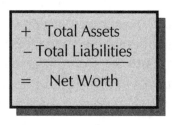

```
+   Total Assets
–  Total Liabilities
─────────────────
=    Net Worth
```

Understanding and tracking Net Wealth is important because it reminds us that all of the financial obligations we make take a toll on our finances. And, it is not until we are truly clear of those financial obligations that we can breathe comfortably. (We will discuss this in more detail later).

THE DEBT HOLDERS

Growing up, my mother used to say, "You can't save other people's money!" Meaning, you can't borrow money from people, and then when you get your own money say, "Well, I can't pay you back right now because I have to save my money."

Your first obligation is to repay the debt you owe. This is why whenever you look at a public corporation that has both equity and bonds on their balance sheet, the bondholders—the debt holders—have a higher priority than the equity holders. The bondholders are a financial obligation while the stock holders have claims to any profits that exist after all of the financial obligations are cleared.

As you read this, some of you may be saying to yourself, "I know all of this. Net Worth is a pretty basic financial concept that I learned eons ago."

I have no doubt of this, but when I look at the statistics, I see a different picture.

WHAT ABOUT PERSONAL SAVINGS?

According to the U.S. Census, the average U.S.

household had a net worth of only about $59,000. This number shrivels to a little more than $5,400 if we look solely at African-Americans. In fact, according to a report by Boston College's Center on Wealth and Philanthropy, we see that 10% percent of all U.S. households have a net worth that is zero or negative. This number climbs to nearly 20%—1 in 5—for African-Americans.

These numbers were based on 2001 data. It would be fair to assume that these statistics have only gotten worse with the collapse in the housing market and economic slowdown which occurred in 2007 and 2008.

With the widely reported mounting bankruptcies, this, no doubt, has probably adversely impacted the portfolios of many U.S. consumers which, according to the Bureau of Economic Analysis, already had a savings rate under 1% and depended heavily on the equity value of their homes in their financial portfolio. In fact, the statistics on net worth decline to an average of $10,500 for all U.S. households and $1,102 for African-American households when home equity is excluded.

GOD'S ECONOMIC SYSTEM

I have previously said that we have to be careful about going "over-the-top" with the "prosperity on over-drive" view of money. However, I do feel we can do much better than we are right now.

When I look at my American brothers and sisters

across all ethnicities, I see there is room for improvement across the board.

Speaking to my friends in the African-American community, we can certainly do better!

The United States is still one of the most prosperous countries in the world, and as Christians, I believe we have the *power and responsibility* to maximize our ability to generate wealth so that we can be "the hand extended" to people all around the world.

One of the most awesome ministries we can have is in improving, not only the economic strength of our own country, but more importantly, the economic strength of people in other nations— wherever there is a need!

The beautiful thing about God's economic system is that there are no sacrifices and tradeoffs involved. Everyone can succeed without it being at the expense of others. We do not have to step on one person's neck and hold them down so we can climb ahead. God will bless us all! And just as He can bless *my* physical health without making *you* sick, He can empower *you* economically, without causing *me* to be impoverished.

In fact, we all have the ability to succeed because Jesus died that we *all* might have abundant life. We do not have to wait until we "get to heaven" because there we can be certain there are no scarce resources or inflation.

The Kingdom is within each and every one of us and we need to do all that we can to manifest His Kingdom now on earth!

TO EVERYTHING THERE IS A SEASON

We hear daily reports concerning the economy. What I find most interesting is that the economy is usually talked about as if it is only supposed to increase. If it does anything other than grow larger, financial news commentators become grim. The sky is falling! What are we to do? The economy is declining. Could it be…it might be… say it's not so…a recession!

We are like the disciples in the boat on the storm-tossed sea. "Jesus, don't you care that we are about to sink?"

> *Now when they had left the multitude, they took Him along in the boat as He was. And other little boats were also with Him. And a great windstorm arose, and the waves beat into the boat, so that it was already filling. But He was in the stern, asleep on a pillow. And they awoke Him and said to Him, "Teacher, do You not care that we are perishing?"*
>
> *Then He arose and rebuked the wind, and said to the sea, "Peace, be still!" And the wind ceased and there was a great calm. But He said to them, "Why are you so fearful? How is it that you have no faith?"* (Mark 4:36-40).

Am I saying that whenever the economy decelerates or does anything but expand all we have to do to grow wealth is stand and rebuke it like Jesus rebuked the wind? No. While, I practice the power of prayer and believe that we should come before the Lord for many things, not the least of which is the economy, this is not my point.

I am telling you that as we work to grow wealth, we have to understand that sometimes the economy will expand and sometimes the economy will contract. These are the seasons of the economic cycle.

Over the last years, there have been *expansionary cycles* and *recessionary cycles*. The central bank of the U.S., the Federal Reserve Bank, does all it can through monetary policy to even out ups and downs. Basically, all central banks, worldwide, have a similar goal. They do not want their economies to grow too fast or too slow. They understand, for a number of reasons, their economies may expand or contract at various rates. Their goal is to smooth out these cycles so that everyone—the government, corporations, and individuals—can plan and manage their financial lives with a fair amount of stability and predictability.

But, they are not God; they are not perfect. *The principles of seasonality, which God established in Creation, applies to everything, including the economy.*

TIMES OF LEAN AND PLENTY

Sometimes we make the mistake of managing our finances—the way we budget, invest, borrow, work, and build businesses—as if the economy will never go down. We cannot do this. Remember, in Ecclesiastes 3:1 it states, *"To everything there is a season and a purpose under heaven."* Our job is to understand the season we are in.

When I say this, I am aware that down through the years there has been a great deal of discussion regarding the *spiritual seasons* of our financial lives. Pastors have preached on going though the "lean times" to make it through to the "times of plenty" God has in store for us.

Once again, while I appreciate the spiritual metaphors, I don't want us to lose sight of the fact that *God gave us very real power in the natural.* Just as there are indicators in the weather of the change of seasons, there are financial signs regarding the change of economic seasons.

WATCH THE INDICATORS!

I remember talking with a colleague in the fall of 2000, as the U.S. stock market and economy was on the tail end of a frenzied pace of seemingly unstoppable growth. To make a long story short, he told me how he was starting to move his money out of aggressive growth areas, to more conservative areas because he saw a number of financial indicators that pointed toward a downturn in the economy.

One of the things he noted was the fact that the *yield curve*[1] had become inverted. Being a student of

---

[1] A line that plots the interest rates, at a set point in time, of bonds having equal credit quality, but differing maturity dates. The most frequently reported yield curve compares the three-month, two-year, five-year and 30-year U.S. Treasury debt. This yield curve is used as a

finance, I said, "John, you know that the yield curve is not an absolute indicator of the future."

My friend responded by saying basically, "Maybe not, but it's reliable enough and, more importantly, when you add together all of the other signs, it is clear to me that the economy is headed for a serious downturn."

John and I then went to an excellent online investment website, www.smartmoney.com, and used their Living Yield Curve tool to see how much the long term interest rates had moved over the recent months. (I recommend that you do the same. It's a great website).

It turns out that John and numerous others like him, including former Federal Reserve chairman Alan Greenspan, were right. The economy was slowing down. Falling off the edge of a cliff was probably more like it!

To effectively manage and grow wealth, we have to spend time learning and watching for the indicators of a change in the economy. This applies to both positive and negative changes.

We cannot be stuck on the sidelines when it is becoming clear there are great opportunities emerging right in front of us. We've got to be ready to jump in the pool!

Our wisdom and faith will allow us to see the opportunities that many are too afraid to see. On the other hand, when others are unwittingly motoring

---

benchmark for other debt in the market, such as mortgage rates or bank lending rates. The curve is also used to predict changes in economic output and growth (Investopedia).

down the broad path to financial destruction because everything has been going so well that no one can imagine it being any other way—(hmmm...does this sound like the real estate market in 2005?)—we have to be able to be like my friend John and jump off the broad economic highway.

WHAT ARE THE SIGNS SAYING?

There are numerous sources we can reference to better understand potential changes in the direction of the economy. They include:

1. GDP (gross domestic product) reports
2. Producer Price Index
3. Unemployment rate
4. Corporate earnings/profits
5. Retail Sales
6. New residential construction and sales
7. Yield Curve or interest rates

For a more detailed list of indicators you can go to sources such as www.economicindicators.gov to find a detailed explanation as well as a calendar of when these reports are released.

I dedicated an entire series in our television program to understand the indicators of the macroeconomic environment.

You do not have to have a PhD in Finance to be able to follow the reports. While there may be a lot of seemingly extraneous information in the data, we can simply focus on the basics. For example, "Is the unemployment rate higher than it was last time? Is this a trend that they expect to continue?"

If the answer to both of these questions is "yes," then we know that particular indicators are suggesting things may not be going as well as hoped for the economy. We then move on to the other indicators and compile a complete view of what all of the signs are saying. Sometimes they will all clearly point to growth. At other times they will all point to a slowdown. There are moments they will be mixed, but that still gives us an indication of where in the economy business is suffering more than others.

MAXIMIZE YOUR WEALTH POTENTIAL

I perfectly understand that some may be intimidated by the financial jargon in the economic reports. Don't be. Finance is a language. And like any language, the only way you learn how to speak it and read it, is by study and practice.

I believe the power God has given to each of us is so great that we can overcome any trepidation we may have—and maximize the wealth potential the Lord has placed in all of us.

You have already begun your journey by reading this book and are now familiar with more financial concepts than when you started. You are well on your way—and there's more to come!

CHAPTER FOUR

IT ALL BEGINS WITH INCOME

For most, wealth does not begin with someone leaving us a large inheritance. It starts with personally generating an income or flow of money large enough to enable us to acquire assets. *(Remember assets are those things that hold or increase in value and preferably produces an income either now or in the future).*

In America, people make money using a wide variety of methods. In fact, there is no shortage of ways. We can make money legally or illegally. We can produce it ethically or unethically. We can make money in a manner that enhances the quality of life for our families and ourselves, or in ways that severely compromises that standard of living.

Our success or failure in generating an income can have such a profound impact on many things, from the level on which we live to our physical and mental well being.

This is one of the reasons why scripture cautions us against wearing ourselves out trying to gain wealth: *"Do not overwork to be rich"* (Proverbs 23:4).

I also feel it is why Satan does so much to stress people in this area. If the devil can succeed in adversely impacting our ability to generate an income, this can have a cascading effect on a number of things—sometimes for generations to come. So a decision to build wealth God's way is first a commitment to generate income according to the principles found in the Word.

GOD IS YOUR SOURCE

And God is able to make all grace abound to you, so that in all things at all times, having all that you need, you will abound in every good work....Now he who supplies seed to the sower and bread for food will also supply and increase your store of seed and will enlarge the harvest of your righteousness. You will be made rich in every way so that you can be generous on every occasion, and through us your generosity will result in thanksgiving to God (2 Corinthians 9:8,10-11 NIV).

I find "the seed" metaphor in this passage of scripture quite profound for two reasons. First, it highlights the precept that the money we obtain is first and foremost, "a seed." It is *not the actual wealth,* but it is what we plant that grows into abundance—a harvest of riches.

So the questions we must ask are: What are we doing with our seed? What are we doing that will allow it to grow into wealth?

The second reason this passage is so profound to me is because it emphasizes the fact that God is the one who both *supplies* the seed and *increases* it.

The power of God operating in our lives is so effectual that it is able to manifest not only income, but also the transformation of this income into wealth.

Let's take it one step forward. Many of us generate an income by getting a job, starting our own business, or both. No matter what path we take, it is absolutely critical to remember that God is really our Source. He is the supplier of seed.

It is easy to think of God as a *resource*—something you tap into in order to meet a particular need. For instance, a resource such as oil or water may be in abundant supply or it could be running out. However, when we speak of the source, we are now talking about the *actual origin of things*.

Man runs out. Earth runs out. God never runs out. Thus, our Heavenly Father is not a resource, He is the Source.

According to the dictionary, *to generate* means, "to bring into existence." So if we are going to generate an income (to bring it into reality), wouldn't it make sense to do that from the point of origin, from *the Source*?

This is especially significant when we talk about our career because we can easily be caught up in the notion *that the job is the source of our income.* No, our employment is *a resource* for our income—what God directs me to do in order to fulfill His will in my life and the life of the company.

In I Kings 17, the Lord directs the prophet Elijah to a brook east of the Jordan River. There the Almighty sustained him with food and water. The ravens and the brook were simply resources God used.

Later, the Lord directs Elijah to Zarephath, where He sustains the prophet via a widow with a handful of flour and a little jug of oil. God used the widow, the flour and the oil as resources for Elijah as well as for the widow and her son.

When we tap into the revelation that God is the Source when we are working on our jobs, we can avoid so many of the tensions, fears, and frustrations which plague the working environment.

People stress over who is being promoted or what business unit has the most authority. Others have fears about being "downsized" or, the current term, being "outsourced." Still others are frustrated by the lack of recognition or reward for their heroic efforts. And the list goes on.

The psalmist writes, *"For promotion cometh neither from the east, nor from the west, nor from the south. But God is the judge: he putteth down one, and setteth up another"* (Psalm 75:6-7 KJV). When you remember that God is your Source, you will understand that the "job" is not responsible for taking care of you; God is. It is He who ultimately makes everything work out.

So when we are at our place of employment, we are not laboring for the boss, we are working for God. As a result, the Lord rewards us (or increases us) with income based on how faithful we are to His assignment.

Here's the bottom line: The key to increasing our income through our job is to do the will of God as we work.

Income Increasing Strategy #1: Master the Art of Value Creation

There may be a few people who are tempted to go to their place of work and begin proselytizing everyone they see because they interpret "doing the will of God on your job" solely as witnessing and passing out Bible literature.

Let me offer a word of warning. If you do this, especially on an ongoing basis, you may learn the hard way that this is not an income-maximizing strategy. In fact you will probably discover this is an income killer!

Instead, I would encourage you to focus on *creating value* for the company.

For example, if you are a project manager, this may mean that you always deliver the highest client satisfaction possible and your projects always come in on time and under budget. It may also mean you can deliver the most complex projects the firm offers— and that you require fewer resources than anyone else because you have a keen insight into the most effective way to leverage resources and bring out the best in your team members.

A project manager of this type is invaluable because everything about the way he or she approaches the work generates profits for the company. When you create value like this, it increases your income in more ways than one. The company may pay you more. Or, other companies may want to hire you because you are so good. Another alternative may be that you choose to do independent consulting on the side or engage in some other activity that monetizes your expertise.

The Lord will use all of these options and even more to increase our income because we are operating according to His principles.

Let's look at the example of Joseph in the book of Genesis. Every where Joseph went, he added value, and God's favor was upon him. What he was adding was not necessarily tied to his working conditions; he simply used his talents to make his employers, and even jailers, more successful.

Ultimately, God promoted Joseph to a level just beneath Pharaoh. He was in charge of all the resources of Egypt.

We can find the same principle at work in the lives of Daniel, Esther, Nehemiah, Ruth, and more. Our increase, the favor of God, comes as we create value wherever we are, regardless of the circumstances.

Income Increasing Strategy #2: Always Build your Skills

Through the years, I have heard many preachers refer to Proverbs 18:16: *"A man's gift makes room for him, and brings him before great men."*

It's true. Your talents can open the door to amazing opportunities. I have found this to be especially the case in the work world. The more experience, expertise, and education you have, the more valuable you are. And the more valuable you are, the more your income increases.

I am often surprised when people do not want to go to a training course that is being provided by or paid for by their company. Increasing your skills is something that you will *own*, whether you work for the company or not. So training is the best of both worlds: it benefits you and the company.

In many cases it can profit you more because the expertise stays with you and becomes something you can build on even after you leave your current employment.

Even when the firm does not offer or reimburse for training, I believe that investing in your abilities is something you should look on as essential. It not only increases your value, but also your marketability and your income.

"Study to show yourself approved!" (2 Timothy 2:15).

Income Increasing Strategy #3:
Never Complain

For the kingdom of heaven is like a landowner who went out early in the morning to hire laborers for his vineyard. <u>Now when he had agreed with the laborers for a denarius a day, he sent them into his vineyard</u>. And he went out about the third hour and saw others standing idle in the marketplace, and said to them, "You also go into the vineyard, and whatever is right I will give you." So they went.

Again he went out about the sixth and the ninth hour, and did likewise. And about the eleventh hour he went out and found others standing idle, and said to them, "Why have you been standing here idle all day?"They said to him, "Because no one hired us." He said to them, "You also go into the vineyard, and whatever is right you will receive."

So when evening had come, the owner of the vineyard said to his steward, "Call the laborers and give them their wages, beginning with the last to the first." And when those came who were hired about the eleventh hour, they each received a denarius. But when the first came, they supposed that they would receive more; and they likewise received each a denarius. And when they had received it, they complained against the landowner, saying, "These last men have worked only one hour,

and you made them equal to us who have
borne the burden and the heat of the day."

But he answered one of them and said,
"Friend, I am doing you no wrong. Did you not
agree with me for a denarius? Take what is
yours and go your way. I wish to give to this last
man the same as to you. Is it not lawful for me
to do what I wish with my own things? Or is
your eye evil because I am good?"

So the last will be first, and the first last. For
many are called, but few chosen (Matthew
20:1-16).

When I began to study this passage, it forever
changed my perspective on work. I know it is a
parable about the Kingdom, but it also clearly said to
me that if I agree to work for a company for a given
salary or wage, then it is my obligation to do so.
Period. No complaints!

I constantly see people who pray and ask God to
bless them with employment or a promotion. Then
when they get the job, they complain about it. And
they wonder why they are broke or why they didn't
get something even better.

The Bible says the Lord rewards a *"cheerful giver"*
(2 Corinthians 9:7) I don't think His reward only
applies to the benevolence that we share at offering
time, rather to wherever we give. And if we offer our
best on the job, then we can expect God to reward
our efforts.

We live in a society where it is commonplace to be
cynical and critical. This is so pervasive that

sometimes, if you are a positive person who avoids complaining, you seem *peculiar*. The job environment —the place where we generate an income—is clearly no exception. However, if we are going to maximize our ability to produce a salary or wages, then doing our job "God's way" or better said, "doing our job so that it pleases the Lord," means that *we do it without complaining*. After all, it is the Lord who we are working for anyway.

When I was a kid, children's cartoons would often end by saying to the villain, "crime does not pay." Well, I have not done empirical studies on this topic, but I will say based on twenty years of observation, "complaining does not pay."

Yes, there may be a few grumblers who succeed for a while, but I have seen far more positive people rise to the top than complainers. If you are serious about generating more income, then be serious about not expressing unhappiness or discontent.

You may be saying to yourself, "What about the times when there are legitimate issues that need to be addressed? What do I do when I would like to have a pay raise and it has not occurred? Are you telling me that I am supposed to just passively sit there and hope God takes care of everything?"

No, I am not. There are numerous instances where we need to address issues. However, there is a difference between complaining and addressing.

Years ago, I was working with a team in Boston. In the course of the project, the workload, in my opinion, became quite imbalanced, and a peer of mine was offloading even more work on me, while his workload dwindled down to just two or three tasks.

I had taken on more work before, but here we had a tight timeline and a seemingly impossible scope. I felt my responsibilities were now increasing to a point where I was risking not being able to effectively deliver everything I was going to be accountable for.

Instead of complaining about the situation, I sat down and drafted some options for how we could re-balance the work. One of those alternatives did include me handling everything, however, I also highlighted the risks that would need to be addressed if I were going to ensure success in that scenario.

When our boss came in town, I asked for time to sit down with him and he graciously obliged. During the discussion, I highlighted the problem and outlined a few scenarios of how I could proceed. I basically said, "I can be responsible for all of this, but I am going to need your help in rebalancing the work."

His conclusion, without my prompting, was to have my peer step up and do his part. He later pulled the team together and outlined a plan for how he wanted everything done.

From time to time, we will need to address things "head on." Here are a few steps you should consider as you proceed. I am not saying that this is the only way. You should pray about and create you own steps which fit your style and the unique needs of your work environment.

1. Pray and ask God for wisdom
2. Be still and wait for God to answer

3. Repeat steps 1 and 2 one more time
4. Devise viable solutions to the issue
5. Select a solution that you believe is best
6. Pray and ask God for wisdom
7. Be still and wait for God to answer
8. Approach the appropriate person to review the issue, your recommended solution and possible alternatives

In Income Increasing Strategy #1, we said that our focus should be on creating value for the company. When we avoid complaining and instead turn our complaints into constructive resolutions to problems, we create value.

My mother used to ask us the question, "Are you a part of the problem or are you a part of the solution."

When we develop solutions that move companies forward, we can expect our income to increase.

Income Increasing Strategy #4: Be Ready to Move On

Once I was watching a press conference with the former U.S. Secretary of Defense, Donald Rumsfeld. During the session, reporters posed several rather difficult questions to Secretary Rumsfield regarding whether or not he should be removed from office based on recent events.

As he was fielding questions, he said something that caught my attention. Rumsfeld answered, "I serve at the discretion of the President."

This statement humbly reminded the audience that whenever the President of the United States wanted to remove him from his position, it was completely within in his authority to do so.

This is the same way we should approach our work. If we believe God has blessed us with the job to be a resource, then this means, we "serve at the discretion of the ultimate President—God."

At any point in time, He may choose to "remove us from office," but we cannot be afraid. We know that Jehovah Jireh, the Source—the Provider of all things—is working everything out for our good.

Several years ago, a friend testified in church about how he had been working on his job, but he received an offer to go to another company. The position was more of a lateral move than a promotion, so he prayed about it and sought council before deciding to accept the position.

It turns out that, just after he left, his previous company starting laying-off people. Had he stayed he probably would have lost his job. Instead he was doing very well at his new firm, far better than he probably could have imagined at the beginning.

In order to increase our income, sometimes God will move us out of our comfort zones and familiar places.

Referring once again to Elijah, we are reminded that God moved him from the "side of the brook" to Zarephath, in order to take care of him. There are times God will move you from the side of your current "brook" to a new place He has provided. *This means that no matter how much we enjoy our present assignment, we should always be ready to move on if the Lord directs us to do so.*

Knowing when to move and when not to move may not always be apparent, but here are few techniques that I have found helpful:

1. Stay constantly attuned to "His voice."

This requires constant praying, meditation, and reading of His Word in order to be spiritually sensitive. Sometimes, we can depend on our natural instincts and reasoning abilities so much, that when God begins to move on our behalf, we miss it.

When my friend was presented with the opportunity, he prayed and he sought Godly council. This allowed him to hear from the Father and make a decision he might not otherwise have made.

We have to be constantly attuned to "His voice." Moving too late may mean that we miss valuable opportunities. While moving too early could mean that we leave the place of His provision prematurely and make things very difficult for ourselves.

2. Do not define yourself by your current position or title.

Getting caught up in the authority of your job can often make it difficult to embrace new opportunities —because they may not fit the image that you have for yourself.

We find numerous examples in the Bible where the Lord breaks convention. Being caught up in the superficial appearance of things can lock you into dead end positions that are unfulfilling and cause you to pass on openings that would not only increase your income but also your personal satisfaction.

3. Manage your finances as if you may be called upon to leave your job at any moment.

One day, I was sitting with a colleague who was extremely unhappy with his current position. Terry no longer felt fulfilled in his career. As he looked toward possible promotion, he did not to want accept the job to which he could be promoted.

Terry just wanted out! He was tired and longed to spend time with his family, and the position just did not suit him any longer. So I asked him, "Since you are so unhappy, why don't you just leave."

His response was, "I really can't leave. I need the money."

Terry's answer really struck me because his income level was fairly significant. So substantial that you would think he not only could leave, but he probably could take at least six months off from work and not miss a beat.

But Terry's case is not uncommon. As our income grows, so does our lifestyle. What we have to watch out for is allowing the demands of our living standard to increase to a point where it limits the options we have to explore new opportunities—which may bring in less income initially, but could pay exponentially more in the long run.

ENTREPRENEURSHIP— THE PATH TO HAPPINESS

If we look at the wealthiest people in the world, one factor which is fairly consistent is that their wealth comes from the ownership of a company either directly or indirectly (inheritance from someone that owned a company.)

So if business ownership is the path to wealth, why don't we own more businesses? Because it is hard! Most statistics only give new businesses a 50% chance of success after five years. Some research paints an even grimmer picture.

I keep going back to this notion of "power." God has given us the power to create wealth, even if it comes in the form of a business ownership— successful and profitable ownership. Do we believe that? Are we convinced that God's power, wisdom and favor is enough to help us succeed? The answer is "Yes, we do."

There are a number of ways in which we can be business owners. We can start an enterprise from scratch or perhaps purchase a franchise or existing company. We can start the operation by ourselves or maybe build a partnership or team. We can work full-time or part-time depending on our entrepreneurial option.

The key is to research, analyze, and select the opportunity that is best suited for you. Whatever you do, never let fear of failure (or previous failure, for that matter), stop you from being an entrepreneur.

A JACK OF ALL TRADES

One of the best ways to generate income and to build wealth is to have multiple income streams. If we have dreams of becoming a billionaire, it is going to be hard to find a company that will pay you a salary of $1 billion dollars.

You have a better chance of making several million but you either have to (1) work there for decades, (2) create so much value for the company that they jump at the chance to throw that kind of money at you, or (3) join a company right before it goes public and its stock price increases by 300%. (I must admit this scenario is much less likely with the end of the Internet boom of the 90s).

Alternatively, if we have multiple income streams we can constantly generate the money flow that allows us to acquire assets.

So how do we do this? Well I am a big proponent of what I call the *Moses Theory*. What is it?

When God told Moses to go to Egypt and tell Pharaoh to let His people go, Moses basically asked the Lord, "And how am I going to do that?"

The response was, "Look at what you have in your hand."

In Moses' hand was a rod, and that is what He used when he went to Egypt—and he used the same rod when God parted the Red Sea.

What do you have in your hand? What do you have the ability to do?

My father was a gifted and intelligent man. He was a master carpenter, a musician, a graphic artist, a boxer, a gymnast, a teacher—you get the point. There seemed to be nothing he couldn't do. For him the world was divided into two categories. Things that he could do and things that he did not want to do because he did not find them interesting.

As a result of his talents, there was never a time when my father did not have some type of income. Of his children, I think the only one who truly inherited his multi-talented abilities is my sister. She sings (opera and gospel), plays (organ and piano), teaches, sews, manages word processing business units, knits, crochets—everything! Likewise, she is never without an income.

An excellent method of increasing your income God's way is to use all of the abilities He has given you.

If you combine this with a little entrepreneurship, the sky is the limit. If you know how to bake, maybe you can sell cakes or brownies. If you know how to clean and organize, maybe you can start a cleaning service, or even a television program on the subject. Perhaps you are a teenager who knows how to clean sneakers to perfection. How about starting a business, keeping your friends sneakers perfectly clean?

The key is not to limit yourself in any way. If you have an ability or something you love doing, turn it into a profit center.

It's all part of creating an income, the key to building wealth.

CHAPTER FIVE

BUDGETING AND SAVING

It's almost too obvious: you must have financial savings, because without them you cannot build wealth.

So how do you generate savings? You need to have a properly structured budget and commit to ensuring that savings are a high priority within your budget.

To say "we need to budget" and "we need to save" is something most people agree must be done. It's a "no-brainer." The real challenge, however, is in actually doing it! And the even bigger challenge is in doing it on a consistent basis.

I teach an entire course and conduct all day workshops on the topic of budgeting and saving. Of course, there is not enough space in this chapter to go through every dimension of the material, but I would like to share a few golden nuggets you should find helpful.

GET A FOCUS, GET A PLAN

I am surprised by the number people who manage their finances by the principle of "I will figure it out as I go," or "It's in my head, I just haven't written it down."

They have a general idea of where they want to go and what it will take to get there, but they have not defined a plan of how to reach the destination, and they certainly do not track their progress.

This is the equivalent of saying that you are going to drive from Miami to Los Angeles with no plan. You know that you basically want to go west, and that it will take several tanks of gas over a few days to get there. You have no map. You have no navigational system. You do not plan to talk to anyone that has traveled to Los Angeles. You're just going to fill up the gas tank and drive, telling yourself, "I am going to *feel* my way there. It will be a great adventure!"

After a day of driving, you know that you are closer, but, because you have not charted your progress or mapped your future route, you are not exactly sure how much further you have to go, and you have no idea of the kind of weather you are expected to encounter along the way. You simply know that the sun is setting in the west, so you are going to keep traveling in that direction.

Yes, this analogy is an extreme exaggeration, but looking at the way some of us manage our finances, this may not be as far fetched as it sounds! If you were to retell this story to reflect how you take charge of your money, how would the story go? Then ask the question, "If I wouldn't manage my vacation travel this way, why do I manage my finances with no plan?"

START OUT RIGHT, END UP RIGHT

I keep quoting my mother, but she had some good sayings. One I clearly remember is: "Anything you want to end up right must start out right!"

While this is true in many areas of our walk, it is especially true in our finances. We can make "money mistakes" that can take us years to recover from. And now it is commonplace to make loans and give credit cards to young people before they have even had a chance to finish college and/or develop a way to pay for these things—before they have an opportunity to sharpen their life skills as it relates to money.

This makes it easier and easier to dig a big financial hole before you have even begun your career.

So what does "starting out right" mean in our financial lives? As a Christian, it means that we base our very financial foundation on the Lord. We then build upon this solid base—the Rock—brick by brick, based on the priorities outlined in the Word of God.

#1 Building Block: The Cornerstone: Pay your Tithe

The first step we must make in our finances is to take ten percent of our gross income and pay our tithes.

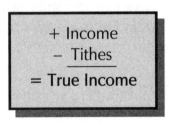

+ Income
− Tithes
———————
= True Income

There is much I could write on the topic of tithing, but for the moment let's begin with a brief, simplified view of the subject so we can understand the role it plays in establishing our financial foundation.

The tithe (meaning tenth) was a special offering of one-tenth of the year's provision. For the children of Israel, the tithe served both a spiritual and natural purpose.

- The spiritual purpose was to give worship and thanksgiving to God for His provision throughout the year.

- The natural purpose of the tithe was to care for the Levites.

The tribe of Levi was assigned to care for the needs of the temple and thus did not receive an allotted territory when they went into the Promised Land.

Let's fast-forward to modern times. The spiritual and natural purpose of the tithes, in my opinion, still stands. Spiritually, we should worship and show gratitude to God for our substance in the form of a tithe offering. Giving God our first—ten percent of our income off of the top—while living out of the remaining ninety percent seems reasonable, especially since God supplied the entire 100%.

The equation could be the other way around. We could have been asked to live out of the ten percent and give God the ninety percent.

Naturally, the purpose of the tithe is still valid. No, I am not talking about taking care of the literal tribe of Levi. However, there is a tremendous responsibility to fulfill the great commission, which is to preach the Gospel of the Kingdom all over the earth.

We are to use the power that Jesus gave us to bind up the brokenhearted and to free those who are captive, to feed and empower the poor, to care for the widow and orphaned, and much, much more.

Basically, we are to do even greater things than Jesus did. This not only requires prayer, fasting, and hard work, *it also requires resources!*

There are churches and ministries doing the Lord's work in your neighborhood and around the globe. We need to support them in every way we can. In fact, the Bible tells us that many of the early saints were not concerned with only giving ten percent. Many gave much more to meet the needs of the saints and the early church.

Am I advocating that you should sell all that you have? No, giving amounts of that significance should definitely be done through serious prayer and seeking God's direction for your life. But the tithe offering of ten percent is tenable.

The U.S. government takes far more than that to meet the needs of the nation; and in July 2008, due to increases in both the city and county taxes, Chicago,

Illinois, garnered the dubious distinction of having the highest sales tax in the nation at a whopping 10.25%.

If the Body of Christ is not worth the same amount as our government, and I believe it is, surely it's worth at least as much as the great Windy City. (*In fact, if the Body of Christ was more puissant, we could decrease the burdens of the federal and local governments.*)

Making the tithe "first" in our finances establishes faith in God, not mammon, as the system that governs our earthly resources.

Hebrews 11 teaches us about the biblical patriarchs and matriarchs who were justified by their faith. It is this faith foundation we build and draw upon, especially as we traverse the economic cycles of life.

Let's Recap:

- The tithe is 10% of gross income
- Tithes are the very first thing that we subtract from our income
- Tithes shows the Lord our gratitude and worship for His provision
- The tithe establishes faith in God as our financial foundation
- Tithes meet the needs of the Body of Christ locally and globally

#2 Building Block: Start Saving

The second financial step is to take ten percent of our gross income and commit it to long term savings.

$$+ \text{ Income}$$
$$- \text{ Tithes (10\%)}$$
$$= \text{ True Income}$$
$$- \text{ Savings (10\%)}$$
$$= \text{ Net Operating Income}$$

I love our country, but on the whole, we are not a nation of savers. In fact, the savings rate in 2006 was reported to be the lowest since the Great Depression.

Some financial experts argue that the statistics regarding the low savings are overstated because one needs to also include the equity in people's homes as another *source of savings*. Yes, it is an asset, but I disagree with counting it towards your saving calculation because, to me, it is not an "apples and apples" comparison.

Cash in your savings account is something you generally can access simply, quickly, and at no cost. Equity in real estate is far less liquid, and it is not as easy to access. Generally, you have to sell the real estate or you have to take out a loan to "borrow" the equity.

What happens if there is a collapse in the housing market, as we have seen, due to the credit crisis in 2007 and 2008, which evaporates equity values?

You can debate whether the savings rate is low or whether it is in fact negative, but the truth is that *the savings rate in America is lower than it should be.*

Several other countries do a much better job and have savings rates that are considerably higher than ours. Smaller, less developed nations are becoming increasingly industrialized, and in the process, their economies are starting to pick up and their citizens are growing wealthier, some of them are even beginning to save more. Yes, they are saving and investing, while we are consuming and running up personal deficits.

In addition, our government is also spending with few controls and adding to the federal debt *(but that is for another discussion).*

LESSONS FROM THE LOWLY ANT

We can learn much from an admonition given in the book of Proverbs:

Go to the ant, you sluggard; consider her ways and be wise! It has no commander, no overseer or ruler, yet it stores its provisions in summer and gathers its food at harvest. How long will you lie there, you sluggard? When will you get up from your sleep? A little sleep, a little slumber, a little folding of the hands to rest—and poverty will come on you like a bandit and scarcity like an armed man (Proverbs 6:6-11 NIV).

This statement is rather amazing. God didn't tell us to look at the tiger, the giraffe, or a powerful animal such as the lion. He asked us to observe one of the world's smallest insects: a little ant!

We see them all the time. And we know that if we drop a morsel of food outside of our house, a whole band of these tiny creatures will begin carrying that food away in no time. It could be ninety-nine degrees in the shade, and those ants are going to be out there working, pulling that food toward some hole.

There is no one ant directing the others, saying, "Hey someone dropped some food. Go find a general so we can figure out how to pick it up. No, move this food over here, and move the other piece over there."

Likewise, we don't have to take the path of least resistance and use the excuse that there is no one who is going to tell us how to manage our money and save. It is not that hard!

Let's start with the basics and *consider the ant—* who just takes what is available. You may say, " I have only five dollars." But what would the ant do with five dollars? It would take fifty cents at a time until it had properly gathered and allocated the entire five dollars. To put it in human terms, it would take fifty cents and pay tithes.

The ant would not care what others thought concerning the size of the tithe or how many others were placing $500 or $1,000 in the offering basket. It would take what God gave and pay the ten percent. The ant would then go back for another fifty cents and would save that money. It would not allow itself to be convinced to spend it frivolously because it was so small. Instead it would diligently go to the bank and put it away or stuff it under its "ant mattress"—not touching the money for any reason.

The ant would continue to build up its reserves until it was sure it had enough to make it through the winter. Only then, would the ant start using the money to purchase some really cool goods around the anthill, and buy new clothes for the Annual Ant Gala! Basically, the ant would amass and allocate her financial resources with wisdom, discipline and perseverance.

This may seem like a simple analogy but the Bible tells us to store up for the winter during the summer harvest time. Like the tiny ant, we too live in a world of seasons—an earth by design. Our years are filled with springs, summers, autumns, and winters. And in this book I have emphasized that in our financial lives, we can expect to have these seasons as well: seasons of abundance, seasons of just enough, and seasons of sowing.

The reason we must accumulate savings and build up reserves is to be prepared for the different times in our lives we must go through. Yes, the Lord will be our Shepherd, but He still holds us accountable to be wise stewards.

THE SAVER'S MENTALITY

First and foremost, saving is a mentality! Most people think of saving as an action, something that they need to *do.* What I am teaching is that you should begin by not doing anything. Saving starts in your mind.

To be successful, you must have a saver's mentality—having the mindset that you can always live on less than you earn.

Let me suggest you say these words out loud: "No matter how much I have, I can get by with less."

I know this is a difficult concept for some of us to deal with because our "want" list is so long. Even now you may wonder, "How can I get by with less?"

Don't worry, by the end of this chapter you will have a good start and by the end of this book, you will be well on your way.

CONSISTENCY IS THE KEY

After we have adapted the saver's mentality, the next step to being a successful saver is to *commit to an amount that you will consistently put aside, no matter what.*

This reminds me of one more story my mother used to tell.

I never got to meet my maternal grandfather, but I've been told he was a man of few words. When he spoke, he did so directly and concisely.

When my mother was a young lady, about ready to graduate from high school and enter the work world, she went to her father with a financial question and asked if he thought she could save $1,000 in a year. He calmly and emphatically replied, "No." Of course, my mom was crushed. She couldn't believe her own father had such little confidence in her.

Some time went by and she graduated as

valedictorian of her class and began working at a nice job in downtown Chicago. She was doing well. The moment she received her weekly check, she would deposit it in the bank during her lunch break and return to work. Then on her way home, she would pass a store downtown on State Street, and would "borrow" from the money in the bank to buy the outfit she *just had to have*, telling herself that she was going to put the money back the next time she got paid.

When the end of the year arrived, she was far closer to $10 in savings than her initial goal of $1,000.

You see, when her father said she couldn't save $1,000 in a year, he was really saying, *"You could, but you won't because you want too much!"*

My grandfather had no doubt that during the following year my mother would have many opportunities to make and save $1,000. The challenge was in whether she had the ability to discipline herself to avoid succumbing to every little thing her heart desired.

Clearly, my grandfather was a wise man because I believe his words are as true today as they were then.

We are presented with more than enough opportunities to save, but we often fail because we *want* too much. It's not that we have insurmountable needs and impossible overhead; for far too many, the downfall is that our desires far exceed our resources.

So how do we become more consistent in our savings? Here is the key. It is better to choose a smaller amount that you can save each week or two, than to try and save a large amount that you cannot consistently keep up with. I have found this to be true whether you make $500 or $500,000.

The Bible has it right; follow the ant and just be consistent and persevere.

It is better to save less, if you can do it on a regular basis, than to save more inconsistently. You can always increase this amount over time, but begin with what you can put away without going back later to take money out of an ATM.

As believers in Christ Jesus, we try to apply consistency in other aspects of our lives. Why shouldn't we be the same regarding our finances? Every morning we wake up and make sure we acknowledge God before we go about our day; and we say grace over our food. We establish a pattern to assure that God is first in our lives.

If the truth works in these areas, it will work in our finances. The race is best won by taking simple, sure steps, and enduring to the end—not just by being swift. As a result of our persistent and steady saving, we will have a better opportunity to do what God placed us on this earth to accomplish.

STEPS TO SAVINGS

We've discussed the mentality of saving and the behavior/lifestyle which accompanies it, but let's get practical: how do you actually save? What steps or techniques do you use?

Here are some ideas:

Option #1: 10% Savings Commitment

1. Calculate what 10% of your gross income would be.

2. Prayerfully commit to saving 10% of your income.

3. Continue to pray about this commitment over the next 21 days.

4. If you do not have one already, open a savings account or a money market account. This can be at a bank or a credit union, but it should be separate from your checking account.

5. When you receive your income, immediately take the 10% and transfer this to your savings account. For those of you who bank online, you can make the transfers electronically. (If you are paid via direct deposit, you usually can ask to deposit a specific portion of your funds into a different account.)

6. Do not touch the funds. If you have an ATM card associated with this account and others, have this account de-linked from the ATM card. If there is no other account associated with the funds, consider leaving the card at home, so you are not tempted to use it.

7. Continue to pray that God will preserve and increase your savings, and give you wisdom.

Option #2: The Ramp Up Strategy

1. If you feel you cannot comfortably and consistently save 10% of gross, then prayerfully set an amount that you can save.

2. Develop a plan for how you will increase your savings over time. This could be over a period of months or even years, but the point is to consistently increase your savings rate each year until you reach 10% or more.

3. Pray and ask God to help you save the amount that you committed to. Pray about this commitment each day for 21 days.

4. If you do not have one already, open a savings account or a money market account. This can be at a bank or a credit union, but it should be separate from your checking account.

5. When you receive your income, immediately take the amount that you committed to and transfer this to your savings account. For those of you who bank online, you can make the transfers electronically. (If you are paid via direct deposit, you can ask them to deposit a specific amount into a different account.)

6. Do not touch the funds. If you have an ATM card associated with this account and others, have it de-linked. Consider leaving the card at home, so you are not tempted to use it.

7. Set a specific date when you will step up your savings amount. Write the date down. When the time comes, increase your savings to the target amount.

8. Continue to pray that God will increase your savings and give you wisdom.

"DON'T GO" MONEY

When I was growing up, my mother had a term she called, "don't go" money. That is money you never touch for any reason. It would have to be an absolute end-of-the-world phenomenon to get her to dip into these funds.

Based on my experiences, life is filled with "something came up" moments. Even if it's not happening to you, you've probably seen it in the life of someone close to you: a relative, a friend, or a person who can have a residual affect on your financial life.

Don't use such moments as an excuse to avoid establishing vital savings habits or to deplete your reserves. Sometimes you cannot be the answer to everyone's prayer. You may actually have to let *God* answer prayer.

I am not implying there will never be an emergency

when you will have to dip into your savings. In those cases, you simply have to use wisdom. What is essential is that you develop the mentality which says "Unless I am in dire straights, I am not going to touch it."

Draw a line in the sand—or the devil will keep throwing rocks at you.

STRUCTURING YOUR SAVINGS

To truly be disciplined in this area, it is helpful to have a structure to your savings. You may have your own plan, which is great. If you do not, here's a way of building your savings so that you minimize the temptation to use it unnecessarily.

SAVINGS STRUCTURE

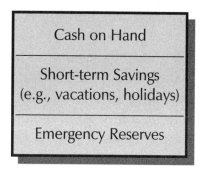

Cash On Hand

- **Purpose:** Is used to cover unplanned expenditures, such as the co-payment on medical insurance, the deductible for an auto insurance policy, replacement of a flat tire.

- **"Don't Go" Status:** (yellow light) – *Cash on hand* can be accessed to cover those unexpected expenditures or help people in need, but it should not be used to finance wants and desires that are going unchecked (e.g., new pair of shoes, special outfit).

Short Term Savings

- **Purpose:** Is used to pay for special-purpose expenditures for more expensive items you have planned to purchase over a period of time. These are things we typically want to avoid running up a debt in acquiring (e.g., vacation, holiday shopping, improvements to the home, down payment on a home).

- **"Don't Go" Status:** (flashing red light) – Short-term Savings should be reluctantly accessed to meet unexpected purposes; because it means that you must start over in building up reserves for future purposes. If you choose to use your short-term savings, readjust your timeline so that you are not tempted to unnecessarily use debt to finance those purchases.

Cash Reserves

- **Purpose:** This is what many financial planners

and advisors call your Emergency Fund. It is used to cover the "winters of life" such as losing your job, a long-term illness that affects your ability to provide an income, and other things that we pray for God's grace to avoid.

- **"Don't Go" Status:** (bright red light) – You should only dip into your reserves when you are in a crisis (a serious winter season in your life), because when these funds are gone, you are definitely like Peter. You are out of the boat and walking on water. As the old folks used to say when I was growing up, we are "riding the mercy seat." If we have to be in such a place, let it be for a genuine "winter" storm that we did everything we could to avoid, not just for overspending and poor planning.

#3 Building Block: Aggressively Manage Net Operating Income

The third step is to manage expenses so that they are less than or equal to your personal net operating income.

If you are talking with friends and family and the question is asked, "How much money do you make?" most respond by giving their gross annual income. You may say something like, "I make about $65,000 per year."

The problem with thinking in terms of your gross annual income is that while it may make you feel better, it overstates how much money you actually have to work with. Let's do the math:

```
=  Income
-  Tithe
   ─────────────
=  True Income
-  Savings
─ ─ ─ ─ ─ ─ ─ ─ ─ ─ ─ ─
=  Operating Income
-  Taxes
=  Net Operating Income
-  Living Expenses and Family Needs
-  Offerings
-  Entertainment / Fun
-  Other Giving / Interests
=  Profits / Additional Investments 10%
─ ─ ─ ─ ─ ─ ─ ─ ─ ─ ─ ─
```

- You make $65,000 but you pay 10% in tithes, so we deduct $6,500 = $58,500.

- You then take out another $6,500 for savings = $52,000.

- Let's assume Uncle Sam takes approximately 30% of your gross income in taxes and other deductions. This equates to (30%) *($65,000) or $19,500.

- So the actual amount you have to work with each year is $52,000 - $19,500 = $32,500 or approximately $2,708 per month. The amount that we have to work with is about 50% less than the $65,000 we initially stated.

YOUR PERSONAL NET OPERATING INCOME

We have discussed the importance of tithing and saving, but now we are down to the fun part—the day to day management of the resources God has entrusted to your care. I refer to this as your *Personal Operating Income (POI)* and your *Personal Net Operating Income (PNOI)*. Your *POI* is the amount of your income after tithes and savings, but before taxes.

Your *PNOI* is your income after tithes, savings and taxes. You may ask, "Why is *POI* a consideration? Taxes are taken out of my income before I even have a chance to do anything about it."

POI is a necessary factor because *legally* managing our taxes so that we are not paying excessive taxes has to be an integral part of our personal financial management. This is especially true if you are a business owner. Structuring your enterprise and business income, so that you are not depressing your net income through superfluous taxes is essential. If you do not have a good tax attorney and an accountant, I would suggest that you find one.

STRUCTURE BUDGET

Tithes (10%)
Savings (10%)
Personal Operating Income (POI)
Personal Net Operating Income (PNOI)
Profits / Investments (10%)

Extra cash left over that can be reinvested.

Personal Net Operating Income is where most of us spend our financial management energy. But, we can be encouraged that God has given us the power to succeed in this area. Why? Because, remember in Proverbs 27:23, it says, "Be diligent to know the condition of your flock, pay careful attention to your herds."

We learned earlier that flocks and herds were a source of income, a source of wealth. Wisdom teaches us that we are to pay attention to the management of this income.

The Lord would not tell us to do something if He did not give us the power to accomplish it. Yes, God has given the power to create wealth, so managing our *PNOI* is just one step or building block in the process.

"IT MAY BE EASIER THAN IT LOOKS"

EXPENDITURES

Mortgage/Rent		Automobile(s)
Insurance	Food/Groceries	
	Taxes (Fed, State, County, etc.)	
Utilities (gas, electric, local, phone)		Dining Out / Entertainment
Medical	Child / Childcare related	Offerings / Donations
Cellular Phone(s)	Cable TV / Satellite	Internet
Personal Care	Dry Cleaning / Laundry	Travel / Vacation
Professional Fees (legal, acctg, etc).	Home Repair	Credit Cards
Student Loan Repayment	Personal Supplies / Bus. Exp. (post, printing, etc.)	

Saying "We have to manage our personal net operating income" is easier said than done for many of us. If we go back to the point we made earlier concerning living in a consumption oriented society, the impact of this is more pronounced in the *PNOI* area then anywhere else. In fact, for many, the challenges, and sometimes even failures, in their finances occur because of the difficulties in managing expenses so that they are less than their personal net operating income. At the end of the month, there are no funds left over to reinvest by placing the cash in their savings or investments.

Each month, they run a deficit and "rob Peter to pay Paul" just to keep their heads above water. In the situation where the cost of gasoline and food are on a steep incline, this can wreak havoc on *PNOI*. So how do we fix the problem and then avoid falling back into this deficit situation?

The answer is complex, but here are four things you can put into action right now:

1. Put God first

- Don't wait until your financial picture improves before you begin tithing and saving. Perhaps you cannot budget the full amount, but do something. Be like the widow in Luke 21 and give God the best you can. Then cover it with prayer and watch the Lord move. Your faith, combined with action, will bring about a mighty transformation.

2. Change your behavior

- Watch out for things such as "therapeutic shopping." Spending based on mood swings and or difficult situations can get you into trouble.

- Commit to only purchase what you can afford. Sometimes, this may mean you have to go on a purchasing hiatus for a while.

3. Lower expenses and eliminate debt

- Cut non-essential expenditures until you can create room for them in your *PNOI* budget.

- Pay off debts such as credit cards and revolving accounts, which can be a huge drain on your *PNOI.*

- When you cannot immediately eliminate debt, negotiate for lower interest rates or better terms wherever possible.

4. Increase your income

- You may have eliminated all you can and cut away all the fat. That's great. Now it's time to improve your balance sheet by obtaining more income from current sources and/or by creating new sources of revenue.

With a total commitment to budgeting and saving, you're on your way to financial security and personal wealth.

CHAPTER SIX

THE TEN CHARACTERISTICS OF CHRISTIAN INVESTING

Now that we have a good handle on truth regarding saving money and the proactive ways to go about it, let's look at the topic of investing—from a Christian perspective.

SAVINGS VS. INVESTING

You will notice that I make a distinction between "saving" and "investing." While many use these terms synonymously, I believe there is a notable difference between the two which is worth discussing. You see, investing requires that you have saved, but *just because you have saved does not mean you have invested.*

Saving is the process of setting aside money so it is readily available for immediate or future needs. The objective of saving is preservation and accessibility.

Investing, on the other hand, is the process of taking money and transforming it into assets for the express purpose of obtaining a higher rate of return. The objective of investing is growth, and often people trade degrees of accessibility in order to obtain a higher rate of return. The only question is "What is the appropriate rate of growth to expect, given the amount of *risk* I am willing to bear?"

NO NEED TO BE AFRAID OF RISK

Ahh, risk—the concept that so many have come to fear, but *"God has not given us a spirit of fear, but of power and of love and of a sound mind"* (2 Timothy 1:7)—exactly what we need to be successful in investing.

The key is for us to look at risk differently. It's not a grim reaper that sits by, waiting to steal your money and your investment return. Instead let's view risk as something that can be easily understood and effectively managed. In this light, investing, quite simply, is the opportunity to generate reward (return) for taking *prudent* risk.

INVEST TO INCREASE YOUR RETURNS

A second advantage of looking at saving and

investing as two highly related but distinct activities is that it helps us view our objectives and automatically understand what we need to do.

If you say, "I want my money to work harder for me, because I would like to have more assets in retirement," your action plan centers on investments.

However, if your objective is, "I do not want to lose my money. I want to make sure that it is safe at all times," you are making the decision to build up your savings. Your goal is complete preservation.

What you can't do is declare, "I want to invest my money where I can get a double digit return, but I do not want any risk that I can lose my money nor do I want it tied up."

This is a contradiction! To receive higher returns means you are willing to take risk—hopefully, only *prudent* risk you thoroughly understand and know how to manage. It is virtually impossible, especially in this economy, to have an investment that *guarantees* a double digit rate of return and has absolutely no chance of loss, and is completely accessible.

If you see offers for something like this, CAVEAT EMPTOR!—"Let the buyer beware!"

Why do we talk about investing from a Christian perspective? It's not that I think an investor can't be successful unless he or she is a believer; nothing could be further from the truth. What I do believe is that we must go about the process of building and increasing our investment portfolio in a way that is consistent with the Word of God.

Start Investing with a Seed

So as Christian investors, how do the principles of the Bible guide us? Let's turn to the scriptures.

One day Jesus was talking with His disciples, Andrew and Phillip in particular, and told them, *"The hour has come that the son of Man should be glorified. Most assuredly, I say to you, unless a grain of wheat falls into the ground and dies, it remains alone; but if it dies, it produces much grain"* (John 12:23-24 KJV).

The metaphor Jesus used was that a grain of wheat had to fall to the ground and die in order to bring forth fruit. We understand that He was giving them a preview of what was about to occur—He was preparing to give His life as a propitiation for our sins, to reconnect us, so we could once again be in relationship with the Father.

It is interesting that of all of the things Jesus could have chosen as a metaphor, He chose to use the seed.

In another parable, Jesus stated, *"The kingdom of heaven is like a mustard seed, which a man took and sowed in his field, which indeed is the least of all the seeds; but when it is grown it is greater than the herbs and becomes a tree, so that the birds of the air come and nest in its branches"* (Matthew 13:31-32).

We see how Jesus uses the seed as a metaphor for His death, the kingdom of heaven, faith and many other things as He attempts to relate to our "finite minds" the *infinite God and His Kingdom.*

Looking at the pervasiveness of "the seed" in the Word of God, we can clearly see it is a fundamental fact that the Lord has established the law of sowing and reaping in the creative order.

As believers, the entire concept of our walk with Christ is tied to the idea of sowing and reaping. We operate under the principle of a seed of faith that grows and increases.

When we look to invest, we have to do so understanding that the law of sowing and reaping governs our financial lives as well. Every investment we make, even the smallest, is God's seed, which—through faith, wisdom, diligence and persistence—will increase and grow.

SHOULDN'T INVESTING BE AS EASY AS TITHING?

The beautiful thing concerning tithing is that when we give our substance, the Lord reciprocates in so many different ways. If we need a financial blessing, that's what God provides. If we need a healing in our body or in our family, the Lord blesses us with health. If we need divine favor or grace, God pours it out accordingly. All we simply needed to do is pay our tithes and according to Malachi 3:10, God opens the windows of Heaven and pours out blessings!

Wouldn't it be great if investing automatically worked this way? After all, Jesus tells us, *"Give, and it will be given to you; good measure, pressed down, shaken together, and running over will be put into your bosom. For with the same measure that you use, it will be measured back to you"* (Luke 6:38).

So couldn't God just create an investment vehicle where, no matter what the economic conditions, all we have to do is to buy a few shares and suddenly there is 100-fold dividend check in the mail?

The Lord performs miracles on many levels, but He doesn't always operate that way regarding our finances, and what's more, this side of glory, I don't believe He *should*.

INVESTORS, LET'S GET TO WORK

There is a reason the Lord gives us the metaphor of the seed. The farmer doesn't just carelessly throw out the seed, walk away and then suddenly the harvest blooms. No, the farmer has to work at tilling the land. The seed has to be planted deep enough and with the correct spacing. Then fertilizing is essential to provide the right nutrients for the soil. The crop also needs water, proper light, and just the right environment.

In a variety of ways, the farmer *has to continue to cultivate* whatever he plants to ensure a good harvest.

And don't forget, at the start the farmer has to choose the appropriate crop to grow based on a number of factors, including geography (i.e., climate, soil, rainfall, etc.) market conditions, personal skill and ability, and the financial situation. So if the farmer is the comparison God has given us, then we, too, must take great care and pay attention to a number of essential factors when we invest.

OUR MISSION?
TO INCREASE OUR RESOURCES

As Christians we have to be serious about being the best stewards possible. We have an *obligation* to apply the same level to our financial investments, and to finances overall, as the farmer does to the field. We are to increase and to put to the best possible use whatever God gives us to work with.

We know from the Parable of the Talents (Matthew 25:14-30) that every person who is entrusted with any amount of resources has the *same expectation*.

Growing up, I always felt sorry for the person with only one talent. But the amazing thing is, God was not remorseful for that individual—not one bit. He loved him just as much as He cared for the one with ten talents.

However, when it came to using the one talent unwisely, the Lord was hard on the individual who had wasted his opportunity. As we see:

- First, God called the person who wasted his one talent wicked and lazy. It did not matter that his reasons for not taking action was because he was afraid. (My feelings would have been crushed with such public humiliation.)

- Second, the master took the one talent back and gave it to the person, not who had four talents, but to the one who already had ten. (Now, the waster is humiliated and broke!)

- Third, He cast the wasteful servant into outer darkness. (Game over!)The penalty, in my view, seems rather severe. Not only did the servant lose the one talent and the master gave it to the person who already had untold wealth, but he was judged even further. Why? Because he did not take the resources the master had entrusted to him and increase it (or at least prudently attempt to increase it). We have a responsibility to increase whatever amount the Lord has given to us. And what is the purpose of this increase? To build the kingdom of God!

WHERE SHOULD YOU PUT YOUR MONEY?

When you talk about investments, the question many want to know the answer to is, "Where should I put my money?"

Have you noticed when you walk through the bookstore or click through your favorite online book website, there are numerous books, magazines, journals, and newsletters touting the absolute best investment for you. What's even more fun is that the answer to the question changes just about weekly. So the absolute best investment for you last month, is not the absolute best for you this month, even though nothing in your financial life has changed. How exciting?

So you ask an expert what you should do. And depending upon which expert you talk to, you get a different answer.

Am I advocating that you shouldn't talk to investment professionals? Absolutely not! I believe you should. But, if you look at the performance of various investment vehicles over time, you will see that their results vary. How those investments perform depends upon the microeconomic environment for those investments, as well as the broader macroeconomic cycle. Depending upon the investment, you may need to be concerned about the U.S. economy, the global economy or all of the above.

How do you overcome such variability? The answer is going to be in how you build your portfolio and how you leverage certain concepts such as diversification. But the way you build your portfolio is based on your goals, your tastes, your risk tolerance, and many other factors. You cannot completely outsource your financial decisions to someone else and expect them to deliver to you a perfect portfolio that will last forever. First, you have to do some work *on you*.

THE TEN CHARACTERISTICS

You have to make sure that you are ready to be a

Christian investor. There are several measuring sticks that need to be applied. What things are you constantly engaged in that make you a Christian investor? What assurance do you have that you are doing everything you can to put to good use the resources God has given you?

Here are the ten attributes you must make sure to apply:

Characteristic #1: The Christian investor understands the true value of money.

He or she knows that money by itself has no value. However, let me give you a little bit of wiggle room by saying it has little value.

If I had a dollar bill and kept it for the next several years, it would not be worth the same amount then as it is now. Money, by itself, does nothing over time but decrease in value. As we discussed previously, the true power of money is realized when it is transformed into an asset —something that increases in value and preferably produces an income.

Money needs to be invested where it can grow, not only to maintain or increase in value—but if it is to have any value at all. This is one of the key mistakes the servant made in the Parable of the Talents. He did not invest the money that was given to him.

We live in a time and culture where there is a great deal of emphasis placed on how much cash we have in our pockets. We see videos of people who have wads and wads of dollars. We hear phrases such as,

"Cash is king" and "It's all about the Benjamins" (referring to the $100 bill, which bears the image of Benjamin Franklin).

Don't get me wrong: cash does have its place in the management of your finances, especially in the allocation of your investment portfolio. But I am referring to those aspects of our society where more emphasis is placed on cash and depreciating "things" than on the God-given responsibility of stewardship and the obligation of building on what has sustained value. Remember, our wealth is not just for ourselves, but is entrusted to us for the purpose of building the Kingdom of God for generations to come and positively impacting others, some of whom we may never meet.

If we are talking about being a Christian investor, one who operates according to the principles of the Word of God, we have to understand that money by itself has insignificant value. It is a medium of exchange and, consequently, needs to be exchanged for something.

Money is a seed, and as such, it has to fall into the ground and die in order to bring forth fruit. It must become a true asset in order to produce a bountiful harvest.

Characteristic #2: The Christian Investor has the right motivation.

Not Motivated by Greed
Some people may be driven to accumulate a substantial amount of money because they are greedy.

They want to *have,* and they receive personal satisfaction from what they have amassed. Not only do they feel they are worthy and have great esteem because of their money, they are constantly striving to obtain more. Pure and simple: these people are greed-driven!

As Christian investors we are not swayed by such motivation because we know we cannot serve two masters: both God and money.

We understand that one of the challenges in building and possessing great wealth is to make sure that, among many other things, our *raison d'etre* in creating the abundance is rooted and grounded in our obedience to the Lord. No matter how many millions or billions we possess, we are still only servants— who have merely been entrusted with resources.

Not motivated by Fear

Some of us have grown up in difficult times. We know what it is to experience extreme lack, for any number of reasons. Perhaps it was a loss of a parent, and as a consequence you had to make it on your own.

I had a great uncle who passed away not long ago. Due to circumstances beyond his control, he was raised by grandparents, while his siblings were raised by his mother and stepfather. This appeared to have left a deep scare on his emotions because he developed an approach to life that basically said, "I will never need anyone again."

He seemed to have promised himself that he

would be his own man, he would make it by himself, and would live life by his own rules. It turns out that he did everything he apparently told himself he would. He built his own business, owned his own real estate, and did what he wanted, when he wanted to do it.

To meet him was great. He was really a fun guy who shared a lot of captivating stories about my grandmother and grandfather. He also could be quite generous—to a point (and only on a good day)! If you visited, he would show you a wonderful time, but don't ask for any money and don't overstay your welcome!

Money for my uncle had become a god to him. It was a source of power and supreme control. It not only allowed him to be in full charge of his own life, but it often allowed him to control others as well.

Maybe there was a defining experience in your early life that prompted you to promise yourself that you were going to make it on your own and not be beholden to anyone. Never again would you be subject to the hand-me-downs of others.

You vowed never again would you have the helpless and often humiliating feeling of needing others—who sometimes came through, and sometimes didn't. And when they did come through, all too often they made you feel inferior because you were in need.

I understand and applaud your resolve and resilience to overcome your oppressive circumstances. However, we must be careful that deep down inside, we are not driven by a fear of "not having enough," or one day "running out," or even worse, losing our independence and autonomy and having to live on the "charity of others."

We do not want to be like Job when he cried, *"For the thing I greatly feared has come upon me, and what I dreaded has happened to me"* (Job 3:25).

MOTIVATED TO BE A GOOD AND FAITHFUL STEWARD

What, then, is the Christian investor motivated by? It's as simple as committing to a mission of being the best steward over the resources God has entrusted to us. The Creator has placed a certain treasure within each individual—a talent, a skill, even the ability to accumulate finances. We may not know why He chose us, but if God places resources in our care, we have a responsibility to do the best with what we have. This must be our mission every day.

For example, you may be a gifted songwriter, and God has given you the ability to write two thousand songs, but you write only twenty. If you were to sell the twenty, make a considerable amount of money and go your merry way, I personally think you weren't being the best steward you could be with the resources God gave to you. If there were two thousand songs in your heart, each of those might have reached a different person who was supposed to be encouraged or inspired at a critical juncture in their lives.

Are you taking responsibility for the talents the Lord has placed in your care?

DRIVEN TO MAKE A DIFFERENCE

The Christian investor is also motivated to advance the Kingdom of God. People around the world are in dire need, and they can benefit from each of us in many different ways. Maybe it's a warm smile, a new school, much-needed medicine, or clean, fresh water from a new irrigation system—the possibilities are endless.

Our passion should reflect the mission statement of Jesus: *"He has anointed me to preach the gospel to the poor; He has sent me to heal the brokenhearted, to proclaim liberty to the captives and recovery of sight to the blind, to set at liberty those who are oppressed"* (Isaiah 61:1, Luke 4:18).

God's Son told us that we are to be the *"salt of the earth"* (Matthew 5:13). He also said, *"You are the light of the world. A city that is set on a hill cannot be hidden. Nor do they light a lamp and put it under a basket, but on a lampstand, and it gives light to all who are in the house. Let your light so shine before men, that they may see your good works and glorify your Father in heaven"* (verses 14-16).

We should be constantly striving to make a difference in the lives of those around us. The enemy wants us to be self-absorbed, but if we become so caught up in ourselves and our problems, needs, wants, and desires—simply surviving and looking out for *numero uno*—we will never get to the business of building the Kingdom.

Our example must continue to be Jesus, who said, *"I must be about my Father's business"* (Luke 2:49).

Characteristic #3: The Christian investor is committed to learning.

It is human nature that when we hear someone talking enthusiastically over a hot stock pick, we immediately feel compelled to run out and buy a few shares—if we have the money. This is also how many of us form our plans for investing. We get bright ideas from the conversations of pundits on the news, but the real question is, do we take the time to understand each investment vehicle, how it is used, and whether it is appropriate for our goals and our situation? Usually the answer to this question is "no."

Our misunderstandings of complex subjects such as investing are further complicated by the fact that most of us were not taught how to manage money at home or in school. Some make it all the way from elementary to high school, college and graduate school, yet they have never been taught the basics of handling finances.

Yes, we can be taught to spend—that's for sure. Maybe we can even learn to make purchases intelligently. Like myself, we can obtain hard-earned degrees in business, finance, and economics, and we are taught about the theory of money and markets. But how does knowing a technical concept such as the capital asset pricing or gamma neutral hedging really help me make a decision such as selecting the right mutual funds in my 401k plan or helping my parents make a decision on whether or not they should sell their home?

A STUDENT OF INVESTMENTS

It would be wonderful if the Holy Spirit would just give us this amazing knowledge of the best stocks to pick, after all He is supposed to *"lead us and guide into all truth"* (John 16:13). But that is not quite the way it happens.

We can receive ideas from news reports and magazine articles, but what we really need to do is go back and become students.

For example, you might want to invest in real estate. Since the stock market bust of 2000, choosing assets that have more tangible value, like property, may seem to be a better idea—even with the home mortgage crisis of 2008.

Once you have decided you want to become a student of real estate, the next step is to begin understanding factors such as:

- Different types of real estate assets (commercial, industrial, residential, etc.)
- Various styles of investing (development, income properties, etc.)

- Valuation techniques
- Real estate value by geography (locally, nationally, internationally)
- Deal structuring and financing alternatives
  — etc.

Alternatively, you may say you want to take a simpler approach and invest in a mutual fund. That's fine too. Once again, you have made a decision to become a student of mutual funds and investing in these funds. So, you must understand:

- Different *types* of mutual funds
- The benchmarks associated with each fund type
- Relationship between the kind of mutual fund and the associated risk
- Techniques and resources for evaluating fund performance
- Mutual fund managers
- Fees and expenses associated with each fund

I always counsel people that even if they have an advisor or expert managing their portfolios, they cannot completely outsource these decisions. Be an active participant in the management of your resources. Never feel there is a topic too complicated for you to understand. Take the attitude that you can do all things through Christ who strengthens you— including understanding investments.

LESSONS FROM DAD

Through the years, we've all heard stories of entertainers or famous athletes who were taken advantage of by an unscrupulous manager or investment advisor.

How many times have we read about an elderly person being bilked out of their life savings? While we may not be able to completely prevent all fraud or malfeasance, I think we can take one giant step toward avoiding exploitation—and that is through being actively involved in the management of our funds. We have to realize that no matter what the topic, we can learn it. This is not only possible, but necessary!

I gained much insight from my father. He was the type of individual who could learn practically anything. Even though he may not have been familiar with a particular topic we were studying in school, he felt that if he looked at the book and did a few problems, he could pretty much figure it out. Basically, my father was good and he knew it. He believed he could teach himself and others just about anything. While we outwardly denied that he was as good as he thought he was—he was little more than average or "fortunate at best"—inwardly he had proven more than enough times that his confidence was well deserved.

My dad graduated from high school at sixteen, the peak of his formal education. I remember the times he sat with my mother as she worked on one of her theological degrees, and he helped her learn New

Testament Greek.

Understanding Greek was critical to being able to translate historical biblical texts, and there was my dad, sitting at the table with mom, creating flash cards and other techniques she could use to make sure she mastered Greek. As I watched them, I was amazed and smiled to myself, "He actually can learn anything."

I HAD A CHOICE

Upon entering college and spending time in other educational environments, I came up against topics that were really hard and quite unfamiliar to me—but I still found them fascinating and was intrigued by the challenge of learning new facts and concepts. Stepping through those subjects, I realized quite often that what I was struggling with was my own intimidation, feeling the topic I was undertaking was so new, so different, that I wasn't going to succeed.

For example, when many of my friends took public finance courses, I decided to enroll in a class called "econometrics" (a combination of mathematical economics and statistics), which I thought, for some reason, would be more interesting. (Go figure!)

When I arrived in the class and looked around, I saw only a few people in the classroom, and none of them looked like me. First, I became nervous. I started to doubt my abilities and wondered whether I was smart enough or had the adequate preparation to tackle this topic. Worst of all, I questioned my background and how it would affect my success in this new arena. Occasionally, I would encounter a look, a question, or a comment from a fellow student or co-worker who was always willing to test whether I was worthy to "run with the pack."

I learned very quickly that I had a choice. Either I could quit or I could press forward. My desire to know more challenged, motivated, and pushed me to move ahead.

I also was determined to change my mentality. The odds didn't matter. Maybe I was one of only two females in a class of sixty people, or I was the only African-American in a class of seventy. Or perhaps I was one of only a handful of undergraduate students in a class filled with PhD candidates. Whatever the apparent disadvantage, I decided to approach it by thinking *like my Dad:* "I have the ability to *learn* anything."

In addition, I began to use a technique I saw my father apply many times. No matter how foreign the topic, he would always find a way to break down more complicated subjects into their component parts. He continued to break them down again and again, until he had the building blocks for learning. Everything in life seemed to be a fraction that could be reduced to its lowest common denominator.

DEMYSTIFYING FINANCES

To sum it up, no matter how foreign the topic of

investments may appear, you can break it down into a simpler concept to which you can relate. This is how we move confusion, intimidation, and "nonunder-standing" to understanding. It is the process by which we find metaphors for new concepts that make sense to us.

The simplified structures allow us to relate to new ideas. Once we understand them, we can reconstruct the building blocks into any fresh or original concept. This is what we should do when we take on any new challenge such as understanding a new investment vehicle, financial calculation, analytical resource, or theory regarding managing our portfolio.

Keep Asking

Another key component in becoming a learner is that you must not be afraid to ask questions. I discovered this early in my college career. After reading textbooks in my dorm room, there were always issues that didn't seem to be answered. When I arrived at class, I would ask the professor the questions running around in my head from the assigned reading, textbooks, and previous lectures. To my relief, I quickly learned that many classmates were struggling with the same problems. However, they remained silent because they just did not know how to articulate their concerns. They basically dismissed their issues and moved on.

Today, I continue this same practice. Once, I was on the phone with my accountant, going through a tax document. He attempted to explain a concept (probably involving why I should feel really good about sending Uncle Sam more money!), and for some reason, I just couldn't get it. I could have taken the path where I assured myself he was right, because he was the tax expert, after all. Maybe I should have convinced myself to send the papers off without any silly questions holding things up.

However, I felt it was my responsibility to understand the information and be comfortable with it. Of course, I do rely upon the support of excellent tax advisors, but at the end of the day, I have to be able to say I did my best to comprehend and comply with all relevant tax laws. So I responded: "I am very sorry, and I know you have explained this before, but for some reason, I just don't get this. I am very aware of your valuable time, but could you help me understand once more why..."

I believe a key component of learning to be the best financial steward we can be is working toward understanding every area of your investments, even if you are already relying on the expertise of a qualified advisor (which I believe is a good idea). If you are raising questions that aren't being answered, maybe it's time to find a new advisor!

Characteristic #4: The Christian investor has a strategy.

If you are going to be an investor, you must have a game plan—a strategy. This specific point was like a major epiphany for me. You see, I thought all you needed was to be smart, read about an investment, then go out and purchase it. At one point, I owned an assortment of mutual funds, stocks, and real estate. I proudly said to myself, "Wow! I am an investor!" However, in reality, I wasn't. I was merely a person with investments.

A strategy fundamentally tells you what your approach is to investing. The origin of the word derives from a military concept. If a military unit has a strategy, it means it has an approach for how it's going to defeat the enemy. For example, the army may place itself in the north and force the enemy to fight in that direction. Then it will send airplanes to the south to take out enemy communication lines and other key installations. They have a planned reaction for every move the enemy makes. In this same way, you need to have a carefully devised approach.

When it comes to investing, your strategy is critical because you need a blueprint to guide you as the environment changes. If every factor remained the same as when you first began investing, it would be quite simple—but things change. The environment is constantly moving, and you must evaluate what is necessary for the short term versus the long term.

There are times you are in a growth economy, and the next year it may be recessionary. Your investing technique or approach should always be evaluated to ensure that you are making the right investment decisions based on the market conditions.

BE READY TO SHIFT GEARS

I am not implying that your investment strategy itself is constantly changing. To the contrary, it remains largely the same; you are the one always evaluating the environment, the performance of your invest-ments, and your actions and decisions, all within the context or framework of your strategy. If, however, one of the assumptions that drives your strategy shifts, then you may need to make a significant change in your strategic approach.

For example, one of the things that caused trouble a few years ago during the technical boom and bust of the late 1990s and early 2000s was the fact many people were using a strategy that took most or all of their investments and placed them into Internet and technology companies. Many did not realize this was their strategy because they had backed into the scenario through a series of "bright idea" investments that came from friends and market pundits.

After the bust of 2001, many people began to turn their investment focus toward real estate, feeling more comfortable because it was "tangible." Once again, however, people did not have a well-defined blueprint that would guide them through the ups and downs of the real estate market. This was especially dangerous because most used leverage (i.e., debt) to acquire these assets.

Debt seemed good because it allowed them to quickly acquire property it would have taken much longer to get, but it was dangerous because it made them extremely sensitive to the interest rate environment (and other terms of the loan) and the underlying value of the assets (this phenomenon is also true for people who buy stock on margin).

So in 2004 and 2005, when the real estate market was showing signs of being overheated, many did not have a strategy that guided them into safer territory. Instead many were sucked into the mortgage and real estate collapse of 2007 and 2008. Because of escalating interest rates on Adjustable Rate Mortgages ARM's), they found themselves on the verge of bankruptcy.

Because of the cataclysmic decline in home values in certain real estate markets, many investors just walked away from the real estate, leaving the banks to salvage their loan by selling the properties via auctions.

A senior partner I used to work for would say, "Even turkeys can fly if the wind is strong enough."

For a while any plan can work well, and the returns can be quite handsome, but are you ready for the market changes? Let's go back to the stock market example.

For a period of time, Internet and Technology-heavy investment plans worked well, and the returns were attractive, but then the market changed. This happened for a number of reasons:

- First, people began to realize that the business models for some of these companies were flawed, and they were never going to make the money that had been projected.

- Second, a recession hit, and corporate spending ground to a halt.

- Third, several marquee companies were guilty of fraud, and investor confidence plummeted.

- Fourth came the shock of 9/11.

- Fifth, many markets outside of the United States began to fall into a recession. In addition there were several other factors that began to adversely impact the financial markets.

I noticed during this time that there were two groups of people: group A, those who had a real strategy, and group B, people who had "a collection of investments" with which they were not sure what to do.

Needless to say, group B lost a great deal of money because, for much of the time, they were uncertain regarding what steps to take. Some market experts were saying it was a "temporary" aberration, like 1987, and we should just hold onto our investments and in a few months everything would return to normal. Other experts were advising people to shift their money to one place or another, but there was really no agreement for a rather lengthy period.

On the other hand, my friends in group A spent less time focused on what experts were saying. In fact, some of them were even critical of the Wall Street wizards. Instead of listening and being pulled in multiple directions, they simply executed their strategies. As a matter of fact, many of them began making adjustments in their portfolios even before the market downturn hit.

A STRATEGY IS CRITICAL

Another reason having a strategy is so critical is that you need something to check against. If your investment loses money, and you become disgusted and sell, what was the strategy? The answer is probably "nothing."

Not only did you fail to have a clear approach to what you were doing, but also you violated one of the fundamental principles of investing, which is "buy LOW and sell HIGH."

Do not become intimidated by the notion of creating a strategy. It doesn't have to be complicated. You just have to devise one that guides you based on your investments, your level of risk tolerance, your goals, etc.

YOUR BLUEPRINT

To make it easy, here is a sample beginning investment strategy:

- What investment will I buy? And at what price will I buy it?
    I will buy selected transportation stocks that

have excellent management and will probably be the survivors in the industry despite the current economic challenges.

I will buy 5 shares of Southwest Airlines stock at $13.25 per share.

- What return do I expect from my investment?
  I expect a return of between 6% and 10% per year.

- How do I define losing money?
  To me, losing money means the fluctuation in the stock value by more than 10%. In other words, if the price of Southwest Airlines stock dips below $11.93 then I will sell it.

- Are there exceptions to this rule?
  If we are in a short market slowdown (one quarter or less), I will hold the investment for one additional quarter if it is outperforming its corresponding benchmark (Dow Jones Transportation Index).

- What happens if it grows faster than I expected?
  If the price of Southwest Airlines surpasses $20 in the next year, I will sell half of my shares (i.e., 300 shares at $20).

You may not agree with this particular strategy, and

you may find all sorts of flaws with it, but what's important is that this is a solid approach for what to do and what not to do, based on a number of circumstances. The strategy also provides a clear framework for education and asking questions. If we were to sit down with the person who created this plan, we could clearly explain to him or her how to improve the strategy. You could talk about a number of things, such as:

- Is the level of fluctuation this individual is willing to tolerate reasonable? Maybe it should be higher, or perhaps it should be lower.

- Given the level of decrease he or she is willing to tolerate, this represents a risk appetite. Is this an appropriate investment given the risk the investor is willing to take?

- Should this person be investing more or less money per month? At what intervals: monthly, quarterly, annually?

- Where should he or she move the investments and why?

A discussion like this is especially fruitful. What will happen over time is that the investor in this scenario will continue to update his or her strategy and evolve the plan as he or she learns more. This is a true Christian investor who is serious concerning being a good steward over the resources with which he or she has been entrusted.

TIME TO LEARN

A strategy allows you to constantly (on a daily, weekly, monthly basis) learn and improve your approach to investing and, thus, the success you experience. If we look at it on a deeper level, having a strategy actually goes hand in hand with characteristic #3, which is to be a learner.

When I started out, I was investing primarily in the stock market, but did not have a true strategy. I could not tell you whether I was a value investor or a momentum investor, nor could I describe my "systematic approach" to increasing my wealth throughout the economic cycle. The only thing I could explain was that from time to time I took my savings and invested the money in opportunities I liked and that I thought would increase. "By how much?" you ask. I wasn't completely sure!

A PLAN FORWARD

Here are some of the key aspects your investment strategy should tell you:

- Your approach to investing
- Your sources of funding
- When to buy

- When to sell
- What to buy
- How to sell
- How each investment fits into your overall portfolio strategy
- Expected returns by market condition

Ultimately, what I'm emphasizing is that the Christian investor always has a strategy. If you look at the Word of God, you will notice that when the Lord sent the children of Israel into battle, they went forward with a plan. The strategy ensured their victory and confirmed they would always have to give glory to God for the triumph. I trust you too remember to offer praise to the Almighty when you enjoy success in your investments.

Characteristic #5: The Christian investor is always diligent.

Next comes what I consider to be essential: you must be absolutely committed to being diligent.

Some people come to the end of the year, then try to convince themselves, "Next year I'm going to be much more disciplined."

They intend to manage their money differently. For example, they plan to pay off their bills, save 35% of their income, buy a home, etc. Guess what? They start out the first week of January with good intentions of executing their plans, but by February they fizzle.

Why? When one element of their strategy fails, they never go back and reevaluate the plan. They don't keep updating and fine tuning their financial goals, objectives, and timetable.

If you are going to be an investor, paying close attention to your portfolio is a must. I am not suggesting you have to be obsessed or worry over it every day. This won't do you any good. But you can't expect your strategy to be a "once and done" matter.

Remind yourself of the Scripture which states, *"Unless a grain of wheat falls into the ground and dies, it remains alone; but if it dies, it produces much grain"* (John 12:24).

Successful investors follow the metaphor of the farmer. They plant the seed, then go back and tend to its growth. They water, fertilize, and cultivate.

We must follow the same plan with our investments. We can't expect to put the money aside and have it take care of itself.

If you look at a sample stock chart, it will tell you that something like $10,000 invested for 20 years will become $3 million! (I'm exaggerating to make a point; the actual numbers are more like $1 invested in 1925 would be worth more than $13,000 in 2005.)

Reviewing any of the markets over a long time period, they all seem to trend up and up. However, regardless of how simple it looks, this does not mean you invest your money and forget about it. While the overall market may have trended higher, certain investments within the market went belly up. Maybe these were the companies you held in your portfolio.

DON'T GIVE UP!

I remember speaking with one older client who commented that at one point in time, she had a great deal of money in her portfolio. The problem was that a significant portion of it was invested in a railroad company which went bankrupt.

Yes, the market is fine, but you need to be paying close attention to your overall portfolio so you can tweak it as necessary. Diversification will certainly help, but it will not solve all your problems. It cannot make up for someone who is not paying attention or carefully executing and evolving his or her strategy. Remember, Proverbs 27:23-24 says, *"Be diligent to know the state of your flocks, and attend to your herds; for riches are not forever."*

Diligence also requires faith. It is easy to become discouraged and intimidated when you are working to invest but the returns don't seem to arrive. You may be trying really hard, yet your investments are not growing the way you want or need them to. Don't give up! Trust God. If we are "willing and obedient," His Word tells us we will reap the good of the land *"if we faint not"* (Galatians 6:9 KJV).

All of creation is based on the principle of sowing and reaping. Some crops take more time and energy than others, but the harvest will come in due time. We need not be afraid. If we are being good stewards we plant and water as we should, but it is *"God who gives the increase"* (1 Corinthians 3:7).

Characteristic #6: The Christian investor is patient.

Again and again I see people begin by investing small amounts of money and yet they want to see their money double and triple practically overnight. They expect double-digit returns every year, preferably every quarter.

At the same time they want zero losses—and absolutely no chance of losing their money.

If this doesn't happen, they promptly take out their money and complain "See, I knew this investing thing wouldn't work!" Or they may rush into the next opportunity that's promising "exponential growth with no risk."

Take it from me, there is no such thing as risk-free investment. They may as well try the lottery! It sounds beguiling to walk up to a counter, smack down a dollar for a ticket and tomorrow morning wake up with a $150 million jackpot.

This isn't reasonable. It's Satan who creates the mistaken idea that riches can be ours so quickly. The Bible clearly tells us that the path for financial abundance is through patience and consistency. Remember, wealth *"gained hastily at the beginning will not be blessed at the end"* (Proverbs 20:21).

TWO SCENARIOS

You may say, "I have children going away to

college in three years" or "I want to retire in four years." In such a case you are operating under one of two scenarios:

1. You procrastinated and were not a good steward over the resources God entrusted to you. Now you are faced with commitments you are not prepared to fulfill.

2. You have done the best that you could possibly do with all God placed in your care, but it is not enough.

Here should be your response for each of the above:

For scenario #1: Repent and ask God to forgive you for being foolish. Organize your life and begin saving and investing as the wise steward He called you to be.

(a) If you have a child who needs to be in college in a few short years:

• Save what you can. Maybe you can cover books, transportation costs, and other expenses.

• Begin looking for scholarships and grants based on your child's interests or talents, your geography, your ethnicity, etc.

- Pray and ask God to miraculously intervene if necessary, but at the very least to let His mercy abound.

(b) If you want to retire:

- Begin to make adjustments in your current lifestyle so you can increase your savings.

- Look at retirement in a different light.

Maybe you will not stop working altogether and instead will change occupations or work part time. With this extra income you will be able to save more money to make up for lost time.

For scenario #2: My mother used to say, "He did not bring you this far to leave you." This was a lesson that she had learned, and as I have lived on my own, I have found it to be true. If we are faithful to God to the best of our ability, He will take care of the rest.

As a youngster, when I was enrolled in a private Christian school and my brother was going to college, our family could not afford both, so mom had to take me out of private school and move me to public school. Unlike my siblings and cousins, I did not have any family members who were close to my age who attended the same school and could watch over me. Being the youngest, I was by myself.

My mother talked about how painful this was for her, but let me share how this worked out. Attending public school, I was later accepted into various programs for gifted students. In the end, I received a private school education in the public school system. I went on to attend two of the most prestigious private universities in the United States (of course, I think they are the best, but I am biased).

It reminds me of a song Debbie McClendon used to sing, "When you've got nothing left but God, you have enough to start again."

So what do you do? Trust God for innovative solutions to your situation. If the door fails to open, look for an open window!

IN "DUE SEASON"

We all want to be overnight financial wonders. We have $50, or $500, or $5,000, and would love to know how we can pour blessed oil on the money, pray in the Spirit, and then have it miraculously turn into a spiritual lottery ticket.

If we think back to the farmers, we see they do not plant one seed and then receive a crop of 4,000 plants. Instead, they plant multiple seeds and cultivate a harvest. Then they repeat the cycle, growing more and more each season.

When you invest, it's going to take time before reaping. Yes, we desire God's divine favor in our financial lives, but we are not trying to exist on a series of miracles.

As Paul wrote to the believers in Galatia, *"Do not be deceived, God is not mocked; for whatever a man sows, that he will also reap....And let us not grow weary while doing good, for in due season we shall reap, if we do not lose heart"* (Galatians 6:9).

Some of the greatest investors in the world are people you've never heard of. They are individuals who have become dedicated to the concept in Galatians—a patient commitment to doing well and constantly sowing.

Here is a prayer you may want to offer:

> *God, I am placing the money that you have entrusted to me in the very best places that I know. I am learning about them, and I am getting the best help I can find. Now, Lord, if I continue to invest in this way, I know You are the One who gives the increase. Over time, I am going to receive a financial harvest if I don't grow weary. I must be persistent and never quit.*

THE KEY IS CONSISTENCY

I've watched so many people become discouraged. They invested for a while, and then stopped. They bought a particular fund, and then closed it. They began placing money in a certain savings account, and then discontinued. They looked for real estate investment properties, and then did not stick with it.

Two years passed, then ten, then twenty, yet they still failed to accumulate what they desired because they were never willing to wait long enough to see the investment through. They never stepped back and said, "I am going to be patient and consistent."

I counsel people that it's not necessarily how much you invest or how much you put away. The key is being habitual.

Previously, when we talked about saving, we said that it is better to save consistently than to try and save a large amount that is not sustainable. This principle is true for investing as well. Remember investing is the process of taking money and putting it to work. So we must choose an amount that is realistic—so we won't have to take it out and use it. Excessive buying and selling of certain investments can result in excessive fees, commissions, or taxes, so we want to be very prudent in how we manage our investment portfolio.

Often, the lower amount is one you can do month after month, year after year. If you believe you can invest $500 per month, perhaps you should consider starting with $250. When you have established this as being completely comfortable, then ratchet up your investment amount.

If you want to invest more in any given month, maybe you received a bonus payment or large income tax return, that's excellent, but the key is sticking to the fixed amount you committed to invest on a consistent basis. Don't let the bonus amount entice you to skip a few investment deposits along the way or, even worse, dip into the till.

Patiently invest your money—in other words, take the necessary time to transform your money into an asset—each month or quarter (or whatever your interval), no matter what! Invest without starts, stops or broken promises. Just stick with it; be regular and methodical.

Characteristic #7: The Christian investor does not worry.

Sometimes when we begin to accumulate a little bit, we become anxious. We turn on the television, listen to the news, or read the paper, then begin to worry about the future—especially if they hint at an economic downturn or recession. What if I do this? What if I don't do that? How is this going to work?

Wait a minute! Time out! We are Christian investors and God is in control. Remember, our mission is to be the best stewards we can be over that which the Lord has placed in our care. Our assignment isn't to worry 24-7 over whether we are going to suddenly lose everything.

Allow me to share a prayer that I personally pray:

Lord, I am going to give it my utmost. I will place my money in the best things You have guided me to invest in, and will watch over these funds as wisely as I can. I am going to be a learner and will study diligently, but Abba

Father, I need Your guidance, because I don't have all the answers on my own.

The Bible cautions, *"Unless the Lord builds the house, they labor in vain who build it; Unless the Lord guards the city, the watchman stays awake in vain"* (Psalm 127:1).

We don't need to constantly fret or panic over our investments or the market. Pray instead. If we approach our investments from a place of faith and consistent prayer, God will provide the increase.

The growth does not come from our human knowledge or brilliance. Neither is it produced by the perfectness of the market conditions or the investment vehicle. All of these factors are worth striving for, but when all is said and done, the Christian investor is marching to the beat of a different drum. He or she is moving forward to the voice of God's direction for stewardship. As a result, he or she should not waste precious time in needless worry.

Characteristic #8: The Christian investor is ethical and acts with integrity.

When it comes to finances, some individuals have the amazing ability to separate their personal belief systems from the way in which they produce cash or what they do with the funds. If their loved one is making money and they suspect it may not be completely above board, they often adopt a "don't ask, don't tell" policy, because they'd rather not hear the truth.

However, the Christian investor does not play these games; he or she is ethical and pure.

In the book of Acts, we read the account of Ananias and Saphira. They sold their real estate investments and made a profit, but they told the apostle Paul that they made less than they really did because they wanted to use some of the proceeds for another purpose.

The consequence of their scheming resulted in immediate death (Acts 5).

The intriguing aspect of this story is that they died not because they had real estate investments or because they didn't want to give all their profits to the apostles. They lost their lives because they did not act with integrity.

Ananias and Saphira had the right to keep whatever portion of their investment they chose; it was their decision. However, they were wrong and probably insulted God when they lied concerning the amount of the investment returns. This couple should have simply said, "Here is a portion of the proceeds from the sale. We plan to keep the rest for ourselves."

This story is a powerful lesson for Christian investors because it reminds us to always act ethically in our financial dealings.

INVESTING WITH INTEGRITY

A popular recent form of investing is known as

"socially conscious investments." People have determined that if the way in which a company makes money is inconsistent with their value system (or their faith) they do not want to invest in that company.

I am not going to tell you what you should be socially conscious about, but as a Christian investor we have a responsibility to place our funds in those vehicles and investments that are consistent, to the best of our knowledge, with Kingdom principles.

If you find that a company you invest in was behind slavery and exploitation, sold addictive drugs to children, and was guilty of all manner of evil, yet it gave you a 600% return every year, then you have a major decision to make. I don't think we can simply go about investing in the firm and marvel at how great returns are such a blessing to the Kingdom.

The goal can never be to make money at any cost. It is not right to lend the Lord's capital to a devilish cause, even if Satan pays a good dividend! We can't brag, "Well, God, I increased it! All I was supposed to do was see that it grew, right?"

No, our heavenly Father holds us accountable to operate from a place of faith, based on His principles. We should not be bought or sold by anything the enemy offers.

We may not always know the details of our many investments, and I'm not suggesting we must go on a 007 mission to investigate every facet of each company in which we choose to invest. However, I do believe we cannot turn our heads if suspicions are raised or if some malfeasance is brought to our attention.

Characteristic #9: The Christian investor seeks wise counsel.

Wouldn't it be wonderful if after all of this learning, patience, and diligence we knew exactly what to do in every aspect of our financial lives at all times? Even better, what if all we had to do was pray for twenty minutes and then receive the perfect answer?

Well, that's not realistic. We must understand that the Lord has already placed into the creative order everything we need. My mother always used to say, "God has already provided."

The Lord told Jeremiah, *"Before I formed you in the womb, I knew you; before you were born, I set you apart; I appointed you as a prophet to the nations"* (Jeremiah 1:5 NIV). God declared, *"For I know the plans I have for you...plans to prosper you and not to harm you, plans to give you hope and a future"* (Jeremiah 29:11 NIV).

The Almighty has already ordained our total success. If we believe we should be defeated in some area, then Jesus' sacrifice at Calvary is insufficient —and we all know this is simply not true. We need to get busy with our assignment. Our job is to trust, to have faith, to seek, and to work according to divine principles. Like Jeremiah, we need to perform the plan God has ordained.

How do we learn what we need to know? How do we make sure we are taking the right steps? King

Solomon tells us much concerning wise and experienced advice:

- *"Where no counsel is, the people fall: but in the multitude of counselors there is safety"* (Proverbs 11:14).

- *"The way of a fool is right in his own eyes, but he who heeds counsel is wise"* (Proverbs 12:15).

- *"Without counsel, plans go awry, but in the multitude of counselors they are established"* (Proverbs 15:22).

- *"Listen to counsel and receive instruction, that you may be wise in your latter days"* (Proverbs 19:20).

The counsel I am referring to are the bright, solid ideas that come along the way. For instance, perhaps you were riding in a taxi cab and on the radio was investment advice from an expert.

I am not talking about junk mail or spam e-mail which tout "BLOCKBUSTER" investment recommendations. That's not wise counsel. I also discount the conversations you have with your best friends who tell you what you ought to do with your money, yet they have no qualifications whatsoever to advise you.

Wisdom comes from training and experience. So the person you seek wise counsel from should be fully knowledgeable.

Yes, there is safety in numbers, but you don't need twenty-two advisors or financial planners. However, whatever advice you receive, you should have your approach and perspective validated by someone in the investment field whom your trust.

In seeking a second opinion, you may learn ways to improve or transform the strategy. Often the advisor may give you a golden nugget or offer an insight that can help you stabilize your efforts. There may also be occasions where your advisor may even disagree, but this too can be helpful. As you build a relationship with your counselors and advisors, you will learn more —and sometimes they may even learn from you.

Countless people have found themselves in trouble because they did not seek wise advice. On the other side of the coin, individuals have sought what should have been solid recommendations, yet it turns out to be just the opposite.

I am a strong believer in seeking professional help (CPAs, attorneys, investment advisors, financial planners, bankers, etc.), but there may be occasions when their words don't apply because they did not undertake the proper research. In some cases, their conclusions were not appropriate information for your situation.

My caution to you is that seeking wise counsel does not eliminate all of the risks and pitfalls we have discussed. You still have to do your own homework, become a learner, and be diligent rather than outsourcing the decision.

"ARE YOU SURE?"

I was once speaking to an accountant and in our discussion, I asked a question regarding the tax treatment of a particular investment I was holding. He answered me, but I was concerned whether he was completely correct, so, needing reassurance, I asked, "Are you positive?"

He calmly assured me he was.

Well, even though I am not an accountant, I had done some research and had made some inquiries. Consequently, I suspected he was not current on the issue. So I asked if he would be willing to look up the tax code, verify it, and get back to me.

I was not challenging him or his profession; I just wanted to be one hundred percent sure that if I had to go before the IRS, I had all of my ducks in a row.

It turned out his answer was wrong. What would have happened had I not taken the proactive stance in my account management and simply relied on his misinformation?

If I were asked what client worries me more, the one who asks a lot of questions or the one who does not ask any at all, my answer probably will always be the latter. Without doubt, the chance for misunderstanding, missed expectations, and misinformation is far greater.

With a client who asks questions, I know that he or she is processing and "owning" everything we are doing. We are keeping each other on our toes and will not leave any stone unturned. The person doing the asking is simply drawing upon my skills as a professional to help him or her solve problems. This is how it's supposed to work!

Characteristic #10: The Christian investor always gives back from increases.

You spend considerable time investing, accumulating, and being the best steward you can be. But if your desire is to just hoard as much as you can, then you're back to the parable of the man with the barns. As he began to store his bountiful harvest, he built bigger and bigger barns, and ultimately was destroyed for his greed.

What separates us, as Christian investors, from others is that we are following Kingdom principles which tell us to give back to the Lord out of our increase. Just as Abel gave an acceptable sacrifice to God from the first fruits of his abundance, we are to do the same with the initial fruits of our financial increase because it all belongs to God. We are merely stewards.

A FINAL WORD

In order to develop these important and interrelated characteristics and qualities, remember:

- The wealth we create and increase is not solely for our own edification. It is for the building of the Kingdom of God.

- The divine law of sowing and reaping permeates our lives as believers, and we must apply this principle as we invest and work to increase God's substance.

- We may plant and water, but God gives the increase.

It is my heartfelt prayer that you will apply what you have learned so that your finances will not only provide you with safety and security, but become a river of blessing to the Almighty and His Kingdom.

On your journey to wealth, make certain you grow it God's way.

ACKNOWLEDGMENTS

I first have to thank my Mom—my mother, my mentor, my pastor, my motivator and my friend. As my pastor, thank you for seeing this book well before I did, and thank you for praying and interceding for it to "come forth." As my motivator, thank you for your love and support in carrying the extra load as I tried to balance the demands of writing and the responsibilities of my multi-faceted life. As my mentor and my friend, thank you for the late night hours and early mornings where you read and provided perspectives on "very, very rough drafts," and while avoiding any attempts to shape what you knew that God was saying through me. As my mom, thank you for always loving me, nurturing me (and all of your children both natural and spiritual) and providing me with such great quotes and life lessons.

To Nellita, thank you so much for reading the drafts, "listening" to the drafts, and providing insightful perspectives.

Thanks to Meredith and Tina for your feedback on the manuscript and for your continual prayers, encouragement and support.

To the Lifebridge Books team, thank you for your expert work on this project.

And to my Christian Heritage Training Center family, you are the best! Without you, "I never could have made it." Thank you for all of your love, support and prayers for this project. I am honored and blessed to be in your midst.

FOR A COMPLETE LIST OF
MEDIA RESOURCES OR TO SCHEDULE THE AUTHOR
FOR SPEAKING ENGAGEMENTS, CONTACT:

DEENA MARIE CARR
FINANCE: ACCORDING TO YOUR FAITH
c/o CHRISTIAN HERITAGE TRAINING CENTER
160 MARQUETTE ROAD
CHICAGO, IL 60637

PHONE: 877-328-9375
INTERNET: www.fatyf.org
EMAIL: info@financeaccordingtoyourfaith.org